Called to Good Works

A 40-Day Devotional

Lorena Alexandra

Published by Lorena Alexandra, 2024

Called to Good Works
First edition. June, 2024.

Contents

Preface

As someone who has wrestled with purpose, work, and calling for over a decade, you would think I would have a lot to say about these various topics, and I do. My biggest fear in life has always been not living up to my fullest potential—not fulfilling the dreams God has dreamed *for me*. From the time I was 6 to my late 20s, I have had various ideas of the work I would one day be doing. From zookeeper to traveling yoga teacher to architect, health coach, missionary nurse, photographer, business owner, etc., I built my whole identity around work.

When I surrendered my life to Jesus at 19 and entered my college years, my perspective on work took an extreme turn. I was constantly inundated with messages about the good works that God has for Christians—like full time ministry or mission work was the highest calling. Convinced this was the only way to achieve the fullness of God's calling on my life, I stopped investing time and energy into my major, hobbies, interests and hopes for my career. I genuinely believed all these things were secular, worldly, and meaningless in light of eternity.

Then during the summer of my sophomore year I got sick with a host of symptoms after a 6 week mission trip. I got diagnosed with an autoimmune disease a year later, but throughout all of it my faith took a hit, along with my spiritual commitments and good Christian work. This led to feelings of unworthiness, loneliness, and a bout of depression. My dream and plan were to do mission work in India and eventually get into medical missions as a nurse, but then, when my application got rejected my senior year, it brought me to my knees. I was desperate for some sort of direction and purpose after graduation - all I desired was to do big and great things for God.

After graduation, I got married, and we moved to London, UK. Instead of working in my dream job, I ended up in a coffee shop running the dishwasher, making £7.50/hr. It didn't make sense to me at the time. It felt like God was punishing me and leaving me on the sidelines of His mission. I wanted in on the action.

Lord, I said I would give up anything, go anywhere, and do anything, but this is not what I had in mind, were the frequent thoughts I had. Much to my surprise, my entire understanding of work, purpose, and calling were again about to be utterly transformed – except this time it was different.

I suddenly found old dreams and interests coming back to life. God gave me permission to dream and create again. I stumbled upon my dusty, 7-year-old Nikon camera and was inspired to teach myself how to use it. I started taking photos at the cafe, helping with their social media, and eventually made my way to assistant manager. I also pursued other various hobbies, meeting creative and entrepreneurial people who inspired me every step of the way.

As time passed, I found myself pursuing various roles to try to find my "one good work" I was supposed to be doing for a lifetime. I worked in hospitality, retail, and eventually felt called to start a business in 2020. Over the span of 4 years I worked with over 80+ clients in photography, marketing, and events. At the end of 2023 I felt the nudge to put my business on hold and made my way to a ministry assistant role at a local church. While I was there God called me to write this book and also revisit my dream of being a nurse. Throughout years of wearing many different hats and doing many different types of works, I kept myself open for whatever was next and however God wanted to use me with what I had.

Many of these jobs and opportunities I held led to divine connections, personal breakthroughs, and spiritual refinement. My work, no matter what it was, became a vehicle to shine God's light in a dark world, and I was honored to be an answer to other people's prayers in ways I never thought I could be.

But *still*, I often wondered if the work that I was doing was good. I wondered if waiting on tables, steaming clothes, designing websites, taking pictures, or hosting events was *spiritual* work compared to people who were in full-time ministry. I spent way too much time trying to find my "one good work" and comparing my calling to others'. My desperate prayer for years was, "God use me in big ways; God use me over there". But what I should have prayed was, "God use me right where I am, with all that I have. Make me your hands and feet where you have planted me."

Then one day while spending time with God, Ephesians 2:10 NIV leaped off the page at me, "For we are God's handiwork, created in Christ Jesus to do *good works*, which God prepared in advance for us to do." This led me to an *almost* obsessive curiosity about what these good works are that God calls us to do. That's when His Word came alive for me as I dove deep into the Greek and Hebrew translations, researching countless verses where the word *work* showed up. I realized that what He calls us to is more than just one singular purpose or job title, but a myriad of good works done in His name that converge into a life well lived.

The good news is that God has way more in mind for all of us than we think, dream, or imagine. He invites us all to be a part of His mission every day. He doesn't need us, but He *wants* to use us. You are not less spiritual because of your job title or more spiritual because of how many hours you spend serving in church. You *are* the Church, and God has saved you by His *perfect* work on the cross so that you can be redeemed and do good work here on earth, ushering in heaven on earth wherever you are. Therefore, you are the hands and feet of Jesus to the people you work with, the people you serve, and the people in your community - this is your full-time, everyday kind of ministry.

Continually, God has deposited in you unique gifts, skills, talents, interests, and experiences that He wants you to unwrap, steward well, and use while you have breath in your lungs. The world needs spiritually sharpened, emotionally healthy, and holy Christians who are passionately and diligently doing a variety of good works for God's glory. As Matthew 5:16 (ESV) says, "Let your light so shine before men, that they may see your good works and glorify your Father Who is in Heaven".

So, whether you're a dentist, a salon owner, an artist, a web developer, a janitor, a mama, or a manager, if God tells you otherwise, this is your good work. But, it's so much more than a job title, there are many other good works God calls us to, which I am excited to unpack with you.

My hope and prayer for you as you read this devotional is that you will come to understand that every single day, and whatever you do, gets to be a walk of worship and offering to the Lord. Continually, may you freely and confidently step into the many good works God has revealed and prepared for you to do.

Introduction

There has never been a greater time than *now* for Spirit filled Christians to take an active role in the marketplace, hospitality, education, creative and entertainment industries. What the world needs is more Christians doing the work God is calling them to, using their unique gifts, talents, passions, and stories for the greater good and for Christ's glory. We can't escape work, so why not let God redeem it?

In fact, studies show that the average person will spend 90,000 hours at work over a lifetime. That's one third of our lives! (Naber, 2021). For many of us and characters throughout the Bible, work can sometimes feel like both a blessing and a curse (Genesis 3:17, Psalm 90:10). Believe it or not, there are 859 Bible passages that relate to work. The word *work* shows up 638 times across the Bible, not including synonyms like *labor* and *toil*. Similarly, if you Google the question, "What is my purpose?" you'll receive approximately 3 billion results.

Everyone seems eager to weigh in on the discussion. Clearly, our understanding of work, calling, and purpose has become complicated and confusing when it doesn't need to be. For a Christian, the question becomes increasingly important: How does God view our day-to-day work, especially for those in secular, non-ministry roles? Second, how do we be intentional with the time we have here on earth?

The conception of this devotional began with an encounter with Ephesians 2:10 NIV, which says, "For we are His workmanship, created in Christ Jesus for good works, which God prepared beforehand that we should walk in them."And as I've been on my own personal journey of rediscovering my work, purpose and gifts I've found myself asking many questions like: What are the "good works" that we are called to walk in? How do we bring glory to God through our work? Does our work even matter? Is ministry work more pleasing to God than secular work? How do I know if God is calling me to something? What are my talents and gifts? Maybe you've asked yourself similar questions, too.

God puts a lot of significance on how we spend our time, who we spend it with, our inner mental, emotional, and spiritual landscape, how we use our talents, and the work we do here on earth. If that's the case, then we as Christians shouldn't take these things lightly, and we should do our very best to understand how He views work alongside these topics so we can spend our days wisely and ultimately get the recognition of, "Well done, good and faithful servant" (Matthew 25:23 NIV) from our Heavenly Boss.

In this devotional we will examine what the Bible teaches on these various topics pertaining to work, calling, purpose, and Christian living. Work is often the vehicle God uses to refine our character, habits, mindset and dependence on Him. Just look at the life of Jesus or David, who both had "secular" jobs that were in alignment with God's will before they began their spiritual ministry. So there must have been some sort of value in that time spent.

As writer Annie Dillard (1989) famously said, "How we spend our days is, of course, how we spend our lives." It's safe to say your work can make a huge impact on your quality of life, and I'll go as far as to say that it can even have an eternal impact on your spiritual life and the lives of others. For some of us, societal norms, expectations, and perceived timelines have tainted our view of work, God's purposes, plans, and design for our living.

May you embrace the assurance that you are purposefully positioned by Him and are empowered to make a significant impact in everything you do, no matter what it is. Truly, there is no greater work than the work God is calling you to right *now*. I believe full-time ministry is no greater than waiting tables, administrative work, owning a business, or being a full-time mom. Your ministry is to love and serve others, tend to your talents, do the work in front of you for the Lord.

Now, let's get into the layout of this devotional:

There are 40 devotional chapters, each with a specific verse laying out one of the many good works we are called to live out. Within the verse you'll see a **bold** word that I've chosen to highlight and unpack as the theme of that day. The bold word is translated into Greek/Hebrew to provide more "meat on the bones." In these devotions you'll find a commentary on that topic, stories, research, and quotes from other thought leaders to further deepen the perspective. At the end of the devotion are a couple of Pause and Reflect questions that will help drive that point into your heart and mind on a personal level. Don't just take my word, continue to study and research for yourself!

The topics are included in the table of contents. You can read this book straight through from cover to cover and implement it into your daily routine, or you can flip to the different topics and focus solely on that area in your life when needed. My goal by the end of the 40 days is for you to have a renewed perspective, attitude, and freedom in your work, and how God views your role in it, along with an increased awareness of His presence in your day to day. I trust that God will spark your faith and lead you to a more purposeful, Spirit-driven and effective influence here on earth, no matter what work you do.

Created for Good Works

For we are his ***workmanship****, created in Christ Jesus for good works, which God prepared beforehand, that we should walk in them.*

– Ephesians 2:10 ESV

Poiema
That which is made; poem, masterpiece

In the Potter's hands, we are being made and molded. Though we were devoid of meaning, shape, and form, God gave us shape and value by His words and love. In the mess, He sees a masterpiece; in the scraps, He sees purpose. Everything He creates, He gives purpose and life to. And the beautiful thing about this verse is that God picked us before we would ever pick ourselves, He even calls us His workmanship or handiwork, which in Greek/Hebrew translates to *poiema* - a beautiful poetic masterpiece. We are His, and He is ours. He had us in mind before the beginning of creation to do good works and *walk in them.*

We weren't just saved to sit around and look pretty. We were saved to fulfill the Creator's intention and purpose in our time on earth. We were saved to be living, breathing, walking, talking *poetic masterpieces* that showcase the love and grace of our Creator to a dark world.

As 2 Corinthians 4:7-9 ESV states, "But we have this treasure in jars of clay, to show that the surpassing power belongs to God and not to us." Therefore, all that we do whether within the four walls of church our outside of it, is an opportunity to do a myriad of good works.

If we view good works solely through a limited lens of spiritual vs. unspiritual, we miss the brevity of what God has for us—to be a living, breathing masterpiece. You see, you cannot separate your being from what you're doing; they co-exist. In other translations of Ephesians 2:10 "that we should walk in them" (ESV) is replaced with "be our way of life" (ISV).

The important message here is that our good works are not just religious activities sprinkled throughout a secular life, as if they are separate from one another. Instead, these good works encompass our daily lives—whether working, worshiping, eating, drinking, creating, or resting (1 Corinthians 10:31).

You see, in Paul's time, the language of "walking" was used by teachers as synonymous to living or engaging in a certain lifestyle. Therefore, the good works we are called to encompass the entirety of a Christian's life—every action we undertake by the grace of God, for His divine purposes.

In that case, Christians have a happy obligation to fulfill the job assignments and good works entrusted to us and to do what we are given to do with excellence, to show His glory and ultimately fulfill our purposes here on earth.

Pause & Reflect:

Do you view your whole life as a daily walk and lifestyle of good works to God or do you tend to compartmentalize your life as "spiritual" and "non-spiritual"? How can you begin to see your work as a way of life and worship to the Lord instead?

Work-Ship

*The Lord God took the man and put him in the Garden of Eden to **work** it and take care of it.*
– Genesis 2:15 NIV

Abad
which means to work, serve, labor, do, worship, minister, and work in ministry

Oh, that the works of my hand would have meaning, Lord. Do I have meaning? When I sweep floors, serve customers, wipe tears from a child's eyes, snap photos of the beauty around me, and sing songs with beautiful melodies.

I want to know, oh Lord, that You see meaning in my day to day. That my work is not *nothing* to You. That my work means *something* to You. Then it dawned on me—You illuminated it—that my work is *worship* unto You.

The Greek/Hebrew word for work here is *abad*, which encompasses all types of labor and service, carrying with it a sense of worship. Therefore, all types of good work are part of Your plan. We are all a part of Your plan. It was Your design for us from Eden. Work is part of Your abundant life for us. What joy, the labor of our hands. *We* are the works of Your hands, and You *trust* us to cultivate, and serve, and create.

Just like Adam in the garden, You trusted him to cultivate the garden, to name the animals with the mind You had given him, to tend to the beauty that surrounded him with the hands You created. That was his ministry, a unique responsibility.

Is it no wonder that this is worship? We do not see Adam sing songs to You as worship. No, instead he worked. Active worship. Work-ship. His work was an outpouring of all You had given him, worship in motion.

So, the next time we think that our day-to-day work isn't worship or ministry, let us think again. God has given all of us a unique assignment: people and work to tend to. What is yours?

Pause & Reflect:

As you embark on this journey to rediscover the sanctity of work, what are your hopes and intentions for the impact your work can have on your life and the lives of others?

How do you typically view your work or vocation? As toil and labor, or as an opportunity for joy, creativity, worship, and ministry?

The Right to Create

Yet you have made him a little lower than the heavenly beings and crowned him with glory and honor.

*You have given him **dominion** over the works of your hands;*
you have put all things under his feet,

all sheep and oxen,
and also the beasts of the field,

the birds of the heavens, and the fish of the sea, whatever passes along the paths of the seas.

– Psalm 8:5-8 ESV

Mashal
Dominion, in charge, has right, in control, govern, ruler

You trust us God, how is that so? You give us the seeds and tell us to plant what we may. Good or evil, yet You trust us and let us go, even if we go astray. You have granted us the right to create - how wonderful *and* terrifying - that You trust us this much with the things of the earth.

It makes me wonder, what is in my hands to do? To tend to? What is under my feet? If not oxen, or beasts, or birds of the air, you have given me many other things: Talents, gifts, passions, dreams, a job and people to steward and care for.

You've given me time, though limited, to have dominion over my corner of the earth. I plan to make it beautiful, God. With this crown of honor, I'll make sure to make You shine. With this crown, I'll make You proud.

As pastor Glenn Pease said in his sermon, *Occupations in Heaven* (2021), "When God made Adam, He made him a creature of creativity, with a desire to work. He gave him a job, to keep the garden of Eden, and to study the animal kingdom, so he could give all the animals names".

He continues, "Adam was made a botanist and zoologist the day he was created. God made man to study and to have dominion over his environment. He gave him both physical and mental work, for both are vital to the joy of living."

If God has created *me* for good works and given me all that I need to carry it out, then the question stands: What is the work that is in *my* hands to do?

Pause & Reflect:

Considering the trust granted to us by the Creator, how does this realization impact your perspective on the responsibilities and choices you have in cultivating your time, resources, and talents on earth?

As you reflect on the talents, gifts, passions, and dreams that have been entrusted to you, what specific actions or steps can you take to ensure that you are using them to make your corner of the earth more beautiful and reflective of God's glory?

Holy Work

Then the Lord said to him, 'Take off the sandals from your feet, for the place where you are standing is ***holy*** *ground."*

– Exodus 3:5 ESV

Qodesh

holy or sacred thing, place, sanctuary; holiness, set apart as dedicated to God; the "holy of holies" is the most holy place, set apart exclusively for the presence of God

The truth is there is no greater, holier work than the work God is calling you to right now. There is no holier ground than where God has you standing. It was not the actual ground on which Moses stood that was holy, but it was the presence of the holy God *in* that place.

Therefore, we are never without God. The burning bush where Moses experienced God's holiness is now burning in us. Are we fanning the Flame? We have the Holy of Holies dwelling within us, His temple. And no matter what we do, we do with God. Therefore, our work is spiritual in nature. Secular work is not secular for the child of God because secular in it's true definition is to be God-less. Catch that?

The believer is never without God. *Imanuel* means "God with us." I used to believe that full-time ministry was reserved for those holier than I, that it was a greater vocation than waiting on tables, administrative work, owning a business, or caring for the sick. But then I realized that regardless of what work we find ourselves doing, it is sacred, it is our holy ground, our *qodesh*.

God is Holy in us, through us and around us. What an honor to participate in the work He's called us to! On your daily commute, God is there. When you're preparing to see your patients, God is there. When you're presenting your pitch, God is there. When you're creating a work of art, the Holy of Holies is right there. He has set us apart for such a time as this, to be all in, in the work we are doing because it is *all* significant when we do it for Him and His name.

Pause & Reflect:

Consider a typical moment in your day, whether it's during your daily commute, preparing for work, or engaging in your tasks. How can you intentionally acknowledge and invite God into that specific moment to recognize and appreciate the holiness of the place God has you right now?

In recognizing that there is no hierarchy in the holiness of work, how can you approach your responsibilities with a renewed sense of honor and purpose, whether you are engaged in "full-time ministry" or in seemingly ordinary tasks like administrative work or parenting?

Integrated Faith

But as for me and my household, we will
***serve** the Lord.*

– Joshua 24:15 NIV

Avodah

Hebrew word jointly means work, worship, and service

"Avodah is a picture of an integrated faith. A life where work and worship come from the same root...So often we think of worship as something we do on Sunday and work as something we do on Monday. This dichotomy is neither what God designed nor what he desires for our lives" (Burkhart, 2015).

Imagine a world where Christians embody an integrated, whole, seamless way of daily living where faith, work, service, and worship are woven together like a beautiful tapestry. What would people say of us then? What would they say of our God? What would the marketplace look like?

"How beautiful it is that they devote such passion and effort to their work as an expression of their faith," they might say. "How interesting they don't cut corners, cheat, steal, slack off like the rest of us. They work hard and trust God to provide for their needs. They even give credit to an invisible God!"

Instead of an integrated faith, we've created separate containers for God, church, living, work, and everything else. As Dorothy Sayers wrote in her famous essay "Why

Work" (1942), "How can anyone remain interested in a religion which seems to have no concern with nine-tenths of his life?" The authors of the Bible didn't seem to have this dilemma, as seen by the various ways this Hebrew word shows up throughout scripture (Genesis 2:15, Exodus 34:21, Psalm 104:23, Exodus 8:1). As such, we must hold our work in high regard, as it is the very thing that allows us to witness to the world *who* we serve and *what* we believe in.

In the beginning half of Joshua 24:15, Joshua tries to distinguish himself from the idolaters. They would rather have served the gods of their ancestors, but Joshua states he will serve the one true God in everything he does. Our "secular work" is indeed sacred, as sacred as sitting in church pews. It allows the world to see a consistent reflection of the image of God. As Sayers (1942) continues,

> The Church's approach to an intelligent carpenter is usually confined to exhorting him not to be drunk and disorderly in his leisure hours, and to come to church on Sundays. What the Church should be telling him is this: that the very first demand that his religion makes upon him is that he should make good tables.

God does no shabby work, so why should we? Go on, work-ship, and let the world see *who* you serve.

Pause & Reflect:

Reflect on your current approach to work. Are there areas where you compartmentalize your faith, keeping it separate from your professional life? How might viewing your work as a form of worship impact your attitudes, actions, and work outcomes in the workplace?

Effortless

I am the vine; you are the branches. If you remain in me and I in you, you will bear much fruit; apart from me you can ***do*** *nothing.*

– John 15:5 ESV

Poieo
to do, make, practice, produce, create, bear

Think of an artist holding a paintbrush. Effortlessly, without force, she begins to paint from the vision in her mind. The art is flowing out of her as she pours herself out onto the canvas. The artwork is an expression of who she is. Do you know someone who is just naturally gifted in something? They usually do their works without much thought or exertion, it just *flows* out of them.

That is the true definition of the Greek/Hebrew word, *poieo*. The common usage of this word during Bible times was with regard to artists, philosophers, and poets. In the secular Greek, *poieo* is used to describe how trees produce fruit (Smitty, 2010). In essence, these are things not taught, but that flow *out* of us naturally, as a part of *who* we are - our natural being.

On the other hand, the Greek/Hebrew word *prasso* shows up in various passages, and is also translated "to-do" in our English Bibles but has a distinct definition meaning "to practice." The visual here is applying physical excretion to an activity or work and making a conscious effort to do those things. These things don't come naturally, but come with practice, effort, and determination.

You can see the distinction in Romans 7:15: "I don't really understand myself, for I want to *poeio* (do) what is right, but I don't *prasso* (do) it. Instead, I *poieo* (do) what I hate".

The point here is that we cannot separate our doing from our being. There will be things that come naturally to us, and things that require much effort and practice. Both are good, both are necessary. But when it comes to living out the Christian life and doing the good works God calls us to do, we cannot do it in our own strength. We must be transformed in our inner being as we abide in Jesus, the Vine. We must become a person who naturally has good works flow out of us. We must allow God to *do* through us. The spirit of *poieo* is surrendering to Him, as we co-create *with* Him.

Pause & Reflect:

Think of a time when you've experienced the flow of "poieo" in your life, where actions or creativity seemed to effortlessly pour out of you. Now, think about what gifts and talents you have that naturally flow out of you. How can you allow God to harness these gifts to do even more good works?

Is there an area in your life where you're striving to "prasso" - put in conscious effort as you practice and learn - that is not yet natural for you? How can you co-create with God in this process until it becomes a part of your natural being and doing?

Co-Laborer

*For we are **co-workers** in God's service; you are God's field, God's building.*

– 1 Corinthians 3:9 NIV

Synergos
A companion in work, fellow worker, to work together

God gives us specific desires, skills, and dreams for a reason, to use and redeem the world through us. Often however, we are tempted to take full ownership of the things He has given us and not invite Him into the process. And when good things happen, we sometimes want to take credit for all of it. But we've got it all wrong: We work for Him, not the other way around.

The good news is He invites us into His mission as companions and friends. God has let us in on His secret plan, and He has revealed all things to us by His Spirit (1 Corinthians 2:10; John 15:15). We get to be co-laborers (*synergos*) and come alongside Him in the good works that are before us to do.

So, that job and those dreams, gifts, skills and interests you have? He wants to work together with you to use them, but we must be willing to lay them down at His feet. And in my experience, He may want to refine or redeem the things we lay at His feet to make us sharper for His service.

I'm reminded of Peter and his brother Andrew who owned a small fishing business and how Jesus used that very thing to draw Peter to Himself and teach him a pivotal lesson. Then out of that experience God used Peter for His Kingdom. In fact, shortly after Jesus began His public ministry, He called Peter to do what he was best at, fish! Peter, knowing Jesus by this point, said, “Master, we’ve worked hard all night and haven’t caught anything. But because you say so, I will let down the nets” (Luke 5:5 NIV).

So, they went out into the sea, let down their nets, and caught so many fish that their nets started to break and started to sink! This was a pivotal moment for Peter in which he was overcome by his human nature, and the presence of God that he fell on his knees confessing his sinfulness. Jesus then called Peter to follow Him and co-labor alongside Him into a new and improved mission, saying, “Follow me; and I will make you fishers of men” (Luke 5:10 ESV).

The lesson that struck me from this passage is that Jesus used Peter’s personality, skills, and business for His glory. He didn’t let them go to waste but refined them and used Peter to build His church (Matthew 16:18). So, no matter your experience, skills or work, God can use anything for His glory, and He may just give you a grand and creative idea to use your work, skills, and passions as the vehicle to co-create and participate in His Kingdom!

Pause & Reflect:

Reflect on your unique experiences, skills, and dreams. How might God be reshaping these elements of your life for His purpose and glory?

How can you approach your work and skills with the mindset of being a co-laborer with God in His mission and Kingdom?

Gifts of Grace

*God saved you by his **grace** when you believed. And you can't take credit for this; it is a gift from God. Not a result of works, so that no one may boast.*

– Ephesians 2:8-9 NLT

Chári

grace, the state of kindness and favor toward someone, by extension: gift, benefit; credit; words of kindness

For a long time my relationship with God was one of constant doing. I believed the only way He could ever find me pleasing was if I did more for Him. I obsessed over going to church, reading my Bible, serving, and finding my purpose to make sure He would be proud of me when He returned. I was a striving child, who had not yet understood the overwhelming and totally absurd gift He died to give me: grace.

When I got sick with an autoimmune disease, I feared His grace would dry up along with my energy to do my religious duties. I had nothing left to give, and I often wondered who I would be if I couldn't give a thing. Where would my identity lie if I could not serve, or strive, or do much of anything?

Then one day with tears running down my face, feeling useless and unworthy, I felt God speak to me, "Grace, your name is Grace." The thorn in my side wasn't my illness, but my insatiable need to strive. And God had given me a new identity that was about to change my life's trajectory.

I had to learn to do away with self-sufficiency and turn to faith. I had to learn that my identity wasn't tied to my failures, accomplishments, my weaknesses or strengths. My identity lies in the overwhelming Grace granted to me without ever lifting a finger.

You see, when the world tells us to earn our place before we can sit at the table, God tells us there's already a spot with our name on it. When the world says to work more so we can show off who we are, He reminds us we are more than what we do. His Perfect Work sets us free from all the pressures of performance – what a gift!

Before we were called to good works He did something no man or woman would ever do. He saved us totally, beautifully, absurdly on that rugged cross, knowing we could never repay Him. God extended His grace, the gift of eternal life, a place in His family, and gave us the keys to His kingdom. But He didn't stop there. He deposited in us gifts and talents and gave us new job assignments to participate in the beautiful story He's been writing.

A new heart, a new life, a new creation, a new assignment. Grace. *Chari*: the state of kindness and favor toward us. Grace is the beginning of our story, but it also carries us home into glory. Grace is the moral of the story.

So, what can we do with all the gifts of grace you've deposited in us, Lord? May we give you a return on your investment, with all that you have given us. Not out of fear, but out of pure love and adoration.

Pause & Reflect:

Reflect on a time when you felt the need to strive for God's approval. How did this mindset affect your relationship with Him? How can embracing the gift of grace help you shift from striving to resting in His love and acceptance?

Consider the gifts and talents God has given you. How can you use these gifts to serve Him and others without falling into the trap of self-sufficiency or seeking validation through your works? What practical steps can you take to ensure your actions are motivated by love and gratitude, not guilt and fear?

Always Working

*Jesus said, "My Father is always at His work to this very day, and I, too, am **working**."*

– John 5:17 NLT

Ergazomai

A verb meaning to work, labor, to perform, practice, commit, do work: it is opposite of inactivity or idleness

It's easy to feel overwhelmed by the constant demands on our time and energy. We may find ourselves exhausted, longing for rest and wondering if our efforts make any difference. Yet, in the midst of our busyness there is a profound truth that brings comfort and strength: God never sleeps, never stops working, and is always active in our lives.

In John 5:17 (NLT), Jesus reminds us of this incredible reality: "My Father is always at His work to this very day, and I, too, am working." The Greek word *ergazomai* captures the essence of this activity—God is continually laboring and performing His good works in the world.

He is never idle, lazy, or inactive. He is relentless, purposeful, and consistent in His effort to bring about His ultimate goodness and redemption in our lives and those around us. In fact, He is actively preparing a heavenly abode for us, as we speak! (John 14:3).

Consider the night sky. While we sleep, the stars continue to shine, the planets keep orbiting, and the universe remains in perfect harmony. Similarly, God's work is constant and unceasing. He watches over us, ensuring that everything unfolds according to His perfect plan. His vigilance and dedication never waver, and His love for us never fades.

He orchestrates circumstances, opening doors that no one can shut and closing doors that are not meant for us. He brings healing, comfort, and provision, often in ways we cannot see or understand.

And knowing that God is always working can change our approach to the work we do, compared to the rest of the world. It frees us from the burden of feeling like everything depends on us, working ourselves to the bone for a desired outcome. No human can work continuously without a break, in fact we all grow tired and weary (Isaiah 40:30) but we can rest and trust that God is handling what we cannot, and the outcome is in His perfect hands.

Pause and Reflect:

What areas of your life do you need to trust that God is actively working, even if you cannot see immediate results? How can this assurance influence your faith and patience as you continue to do the work, but entrust the outcome to Him?

God Ordained Stations

"As a prisoner for the Lord, then, I urge you to live a life worthy of the calling you have received."

– Ephesians 4:1 NIV

Klesis
Call, calling; situation, station in life: – called

What is your calling? That's a big question, isn't it? But the word "calling" used in Ephesians 4:1 translates to the Greek word *klesis*, which means situation or station in life. So instead, the question becomes, what is your current station in life? Where does God want you to set up camp for a season? Maybe, just maybe, the thing God is calling you to do is right in front of you.

So often, we are consumed with the future, when God is asking us to be present in the here and now. We desire the "greater glory" days ahead instead of the greatness in today. He has given us blessings, responsibilities, and good works that He has already prepared for us *right now*. And often we miss the good in today, because we think tomorrow will be better. But the greater glory days can only come when we do the small things faithfully.

As Christine Caine so passionately preached in her sermon *Steps of Faith - Small Beginnings* (2024), "Start living on assignment right where you are, with what you have, with whom you are around... That's how you step into your God-given purpose."

Many of the people I look up to who are doing the things I dream of started in small places and small stations, doing "small" things. They were faithful in the stations of their life *before* God increased the size of their station, or upgraded them to a new and bigger one.

They did the *next right thing* with faith and obedience, when many people wouldn't even show up. They did dirty, difficult, unseen work and continued to show up when others would quit. They made the time in their station worthwhile and beautiful until their next assignment. And many of us may have multiple callings and various vocations that we will step into in our lives before we fully arrive to the vision we have in mind.

In general, people lump calling, job, and career under "vocation.", but Martin Luther, the great Protestant Reformer, redefined the idea of vocation: "Luther used the German word *Beruf* to mean occupation, but enlarged the meaning to include multiple positions that people occupy during their life on earth: biological (father, mother, son, wife, etc.), social (master, servant, laborer, etc.), and community (officeholder, church leader, volunteer, etc.)" (Snodgrass, 2022).

This should be a freeing perspective for those who may have not "found" their calling, as if it's something we merely stumble upon while others are lucky to have found theirs. Instead, we are already in our current life stations because that is where God wants us for a season, or until our time on earth ends.

So today, how can you remain steadfast and faithful in the stations God has put you in, with the people around you, and the work you're already doing? Because you never know when God will change things up and usher you into the next season, or *station* of life.

Pause & Reflect:

Reflect on your current station in life. What blessings, responsibilities, and people has God placed in your life? How can you be more present and intentional in the here and now, recognizing that God has given you your stations in life?

Explore the idea of vocation and calling as encompassing various roles and positions in life. In what ways can you view your biological, social, and community roles as part of your calling, recognizing that each has its unique significance and purpose?

The Small Things

He has shown you, O mortal, what is good. And what does the LORD ***require*** *of you? To act justly and to love mercy and to walk humbly with your God.*

– Micah 6:8 NIV

Daras

to seek, inquire, consult; to ponder, be sought after; to let oneself be inquired of, to allow a search to be made

We often over-complicate our purpose and callings. We may think there is something grand and obscure we must be doing with our lives that we haven't yet discovered. When we see pastors, missionaries, speakers, authors, CEOs, and leaders on the front lines, we may think that God is overlooking us. We may wonder why we haven't yet found our "thing." But we forget that it's the small things overtime, that lead to bigger things. The small things are just as important.

It's great to have big aspirations, dreams, and desires to make an impact, but what if the good works and purposes God requires of us are much simpler than we think? The word "require" in Micah 6:8 translates to the Greek word *daras,* meaning to inquire, seek after and search for. God is seeking and inquiring from us to do good, and guess what? There are many good things we can do while we wait to discover our specific purpose or calling. In fact, there are over 613 commands in the Bible!

So, what if we don't have to turn over every rock to find our calling because God has given us the blueprint of multiple good works in His word? And what if when we seek Him and commit to doing a few "small" requirements each week, or each month, we find that it grows and grows into a life well-lived for the Lord.

Simple actions and habits done consistently and by God's help over time, lead to powerful results and a transformed inward being.

Here is a list of "small" things to start with:

Pray consistently.
Be holy.
Give generously.
Be gentle.
Do not lie.
Be angry and do not sin.
Do not be lazy.
Be humble.

These things may seem insignificant to us in comparison to grand obscure things like flying to the moon, reversing poverty, finding a cure for cancer, or converting thousands to Christ. But God counts the small things, too. In fact it says, "whoever is faithful with very little will also be faithful with much, and whoever is dishonest with very little will also be dishonest with much" (Luke 16:10 BSB).

So, what if the "small" things, like loving your neighbor, forgiving others, holding your tongue, and *being* like Christ are the good works that can change the world? What if the small, day-to-day living and obedience is the first step to transforming us inwardly which is a requirement before we do bigger things? What if we don't need to achieve grand things to live an abundant life for the Lord because the small things done with love can be felt by others? As Brother Lawrence (1982) said, "We ought not to be weary of doing little things for the love of God, who regards not the greatness of the work, but the love with which it is performed."

Pause & Reflect:

Reflect on Micah 6:8 and the simplicity of the Lord's good works for us. How can you intentionally incorporate 1-2 simple, yet powerful commands into your daily life, and what impact might they have on your journey toward fulfilling your bigger purpose?

Think about it: If God were to usher you into your next big assignment today, would you be ready? Or are there some smaller requirements, godly attributes and habits you can work on in this season that can prepare you for much bigger requirements in the next?

True Success

*For this is God's will, your **sanctification**...*

– 1 Thessalonians 4:3 ESV

Hagiasmos
holiness, holy, sanctifying work, sanctified, set apart

When I was 21 I prayed desperately for God to reveal His purpose and will for my life, and finally these words flew off the page and hit me: "For this is God's will, your sanctification..." (1 Thessalonians 4:3 ESV). The Message version says: "Keep on doing what we told you to do to please God, not in a dogged religious plod, but in a living, spirited dance."

It felt so simple...to keep on doing what He had revealed for me to do, to keep becoming more like Him, to keep following His commands. I felt the weight of figuring out what to do with my life lift off of my shoulders. You see, I believe God cares so much more about our inward being and character - our inner landscape - than the outward doing of our hands. Scripture reminds us that God doesn't see as man sees (1 Samuel 16:7). Success to us is not the same as success to the living God.

We place worth on finished check lists, mile long resumes, money in the bank, a well-kept home, a flourishing career, serving countless hours in church. But God looks inwardly at the heart, our motives, our *being*. And I've learned that God often wants me to *become*, inwardly, before I *do,* outwardly - otherwise there's a lack of integration, effectiveness and/or fruitfulness in the outcome.

Maybe your whole identity and idea of success has been placed at the altar of work, accomplishment, and striving to gain applause or approval. While it's not wrong to want to succeed or accomplish things in life, we should never try to substitute these things in place of an intimate relationship with Christ who gives us all that we long for.

Many of us are spreading ourselves thin to please others or appease a religion. But let us not be stretched five feet wide with our work and schedules, and only five inches deep with our Heavenly Father. Let us live and move and become like Him in all things, because *sanctification* is the true success we desire.

Sanctification in Greek translates to *hagiasmos* which is the state or process of being made holy. It also means "to set apart for special use or purpose". Therefore, God's greatest will for our lives is to enter the secret place, and first and foremost to know Him and be loved by Him. From there, as we continue to surrender to Him, we become transformed in every way, and the good works become second nature. And how do we become sanctified; you may ask?

Well, I believe God uses different things to sanctify each one of us. We can become sanctified through our work, relationships, suffering, trials, successes, or losses. And these things in unison with seeking His presence and His word will refine our character, our faith and our devotions, which can ultimately lead to effectiveness and fruitfulness in our actions and the work we set out to do. Are we allowing ourselves to be set apart for Him first, and our doing second?

Pause & Reflect:

What is your view of success in life? How much value do you place on external accomplishments and achievements in defining your success and worth? Consider instead what God may view as success and whether you may have unintentionally prioritized the "doing" over the "being."

Consider the balance between spreading yourself thin with external tasks and deepening your relationship with God. Are there areas in your life where you've prioritized busyness at the expense of a deeper connection with the Lord? How can you shift your focus to live, move, and become more like Him in all things (Acts 17:28)?

Meant to Shine

You are the light of the world. A town built on a hill cannot be hidden. Neither do people light a lamp and put it under a bowl. Instead they put it on its stand, and it gives light to everyone in the house. In the same way, let your light shine before others, that they may see your good works and glorify your Father in heaven.

--Matthew 5:14-16 NIV

Phos

Light, daylight, anything emitting light, that which is exposed to the view of all, openly, publicly

Lord, You spoke light into being by a single word. We become what we believe, do, and see - like becomes like. If you are Light, then we become like You, the longer we linger in Your presence.

You permeate our hearts and minds and expose the dark without fear of what's hidden. Your light is like a magnet - or repellant - calling us forward to find mercy in time of need or for some to hide and run, becoming small.

You call us to shine without fear of who will see us. You have appointed us, destined us, set us apart, to be Your lighthouse, harbor, a guiding light to those who are lost in a sea of darkness.

Too many of us try to hide, but God's children are *meant* to shine. You set us as a city on a hill for us to be seen because You first saw us - naked, vulnerable, ashamed - yet still fully loved. A city on a hill emits its light to all, but why are we afraid to be seen? To speak up? To speak truth? Is it people's opinions? Criticisms? Rejection?

God wants us on full display, permeating His light and glory in all our being and our doing, convincing others who don't know of His beauty. You see, when Jesus says we are the light of the world, that a city on a hill cannot be hidden, and that our light must shine, that means we cannot passively sit on the gifts, stories, and good works He has given us.

We are called to shine forth, and this happens naturally as an overflow, drawing ever nearer to Him. We shine differently than the world, not to gain popularity, please others, or prove our worth - but we shine for Him so that *He* is glorified.

And the beautiful thing is, we can't all shine in the same place before the same people. We must shine where God has us, in our own unique way. So shine, and keep on shining. Let us set the world ablaze with the Light of the World.

Pause & Reflect:

Consider the idea of being appointed, destined, and set apart as a lighthouse, harbor, and guiding light in the midst of darkness. How does this perspective impact your understanding of your purpose and the responsibility to shine your light in the unique place and manner where God has placed you?

Explore any fears or hesitations you may have about shining your light, whether due to concerns about opinions, criticisms, false projections, or rejection. How can knowing God's love and approval help you overcome these fears and embrace the call to shine without reservation?

Joint Participation

*And have no **fellowship** with the unfruitful works of darkness, but rather expose them. For it is shameful even to speak of those things which are done by them in secret.*

– Ephesians 5:11,12 NKJV

Koinonia

which refers to concepts such as fellowship, joint participation, partnership, intimacy, a gift jointly contributed, a collection.

Among the many good works we are created for, one of them, though not least, is exposing falsehood and evil deeds. Every day we have an opportunity to have active participation in good deeds, or the deeds of darkness.

We can hold hands with the devil, whose goal is our destruction, or hold hands with the Holy One, who wants restoration. One little lie, one hateful comment, one selfish action is a seed we sow that keeps on growing - if we let it. In the end there is no harvest, just a garden of weeds - unfruitful to all those who eat of it.

Our job is to invite others to participate in the works that bear much fruit. A little good here, a little good there, our harvest grows and grows and benefits mankind. That's the heart of the Greek/Hebrew word *koinonia*: joint participation with God and others in good works. It evokes a communion that is intimate and close-knit, like a wife and husband.

How does this apply to our work? Well, think about your workplace. What are the things people do there that are not glorifying to God? Gossiping, slacking off, manipulating, lying, stealing, abusing others?

Now, think of the way you can be different and set apart as God's instrument for good. You may not be popular or well-liked if you don't knit yourself in with sin, in fact people may mock you, gossip about you and avoid you (1 Peter 4:4), but you will be closeknit with God and His family, and that my friends, is a better outcome.

So, let us not have fellowship with works of the flesh or evil pursuits that promise some sort of good. Our only work is to do the work of Him who called us. When we join in His partnership, our Master will give us a share in everything in the afterlife (Matthew 25:21).

As Martin Luther King Jr. (1957) famously said, "Darkness cannot drive out darkness: only light can do that. Hate cannot drive out hate: only love can do that." Choose to be the light and have sweet fellowship with Goodness.

Pause & Reflect:

Consider the analogy of sowing seeds with our actions, where one lie, hateful comment, or selfish action can grow into a garden of weeds. How does this imagery impact your awareness of the consequences of your words and actions? In what ways can you be intentional about sowing seeds that bear much fruit in your relationships and community?

Rewards

Whatever you do, work at it with all your heart, as working for the Lord, not for human masters, since you know that you will receive an inheritance from the Lord as a ***reward****. It is the Lord Christ you are serving.*

– Colossians 3:23-24

Antapodosis

Reward, repayment, recompense, pay back

The Lord convicted me during a season of doing "unseen" work day in and day out. I was used to being the center of attention, popular and well-liked by many. My work was often seen by others and my reward was other's approval, applause and attention. As He transitioned me out of visibility to keeping a low profile, He started to reveal my motives for wanting to do good works in the first place. I began questioning if my pursuit of validation was my sole focus, and if I never received a single ounce of "eye-service" or applause, would I still work hard and do good?

In Ephesians 6:6 (ESV) we are reminded to not just work hard "in the way of eyeservice, as men-pleasers; but as servants of Christ, doing the will of God from the heart". 2 Chronicles 15:7 (ASV) also says to "not let our hands be slack; for our work shall be rewarded".

The word "reward" used in these verses translates to the Greek/Hebrew word *antapodosis*, meaning to richly reward services rendered, or pay back. The Bible often speaks about hard work, dedication and blessings or rewards. The rewards and blessings we receive are often dependent on our obedience, motives and what we sow, whether from the flesh or from the Spirit (Galatians 6:7-9).

It struck me one day while reading Matthew 6:2 (NIV):

"So when you give to the needy, do not announce it with trumpets, as the hypocrites do in the synagogues and on the streets, to be honored by others. ***Truly I tell you, they have received their reward in full.*** *But when you give to the needy, do not let your left hand know what your right hand is doing, so that your giving may be in secret.* ***Then your Father, who sees what is done in secret, will reward you."***

I then realized that if I was only doing things to please others, or receive some sort of praise and external validation, that I had already received the reward in full, and as shallow and fleeting as it may be, it would never be enough. God was teaching me instead, to seek the rewards that He alone can give, which are sufficient, eternal and long-lasting, but this required doing work in secret, knowing I wouldn't always be seen or praised by man.

Was I willing to make the shift? This experience changed my whole approach to hard work and rewards, and the motives I often had for chasing after certain careers, creative projects and so on. God is watching at all times, whether we realize it or not, and He sees the intentions and desires of our hearts.

Note that it's not wrong to *want* to be rewarded for your efforts, it's merely a part of being human! And throughout scripture God loves to reward those who have faith, fulfill their service and are obedient. And when we switch our perspective from being people-pleasers to God-pleasers, doing our work humbly and wholeheartedly, we can rest assured that the Lord acknowledges our efforts and promises to reward us in a much greater way (Matthew 6:3-4). These rewards can come in various forms; physical, material, emotional, relational, or spiritual. They can come in this life, or *after*.

Ultimately, God is unlike our earthly employers. He is a good Boss, not shrewd, neglectful, or aloof. Every assignment, every interaction, every task becomes an opportunity to glorify the Lord. He sees our hard work and efforts when others overlook us. He sees the things we do in secret, whether good or bad. He sees when we do things others neglect without supervision, when we go the extra mile even if we never receive praise. And in the end, we must remember that we have already won, because our ultimate reward is not with man, but with Jesus Christ. So, what reward do you seek?

Pause & Reflect:

How does the idea of working for the Lord, rather than human masters, reshape your perspective on the daily tasks and responsibilities you face in your work or daily life?

Reflect on a specific task or project you're currently working on. In what ways can you approach it with all your heart, as an offering to the Lord? How might your attitude and approach change if you consider it a form of worship?

Representative

And whatever you do, whether in word of deed, do it all in the name of the Lord Jesus, giving thanks through him to God the Father.

– Colossians 3:17 NIV

Onoma

name, title, reputation, representative, a person chosen or appointed to act or speak on behalf of another

Just perform a quick scroll on Instagram, Facebook or TikTok and you'll find thousands of brand ambassadors and influencers trying to sell you on a product or service. In essence, brand ambassadors are people who represent and market a company, its services or products and act as the embodiment of the company's brand and values.

When you think about your words and deeds, and the work you do, are you representing Jesus well? We are the brand ambassadors appointed to represent, speak, and act on behalf of Jesus Christ—the King! In business terms, He is our CEO, and we are His employees, doing good in His name. Whatever we say, do, or ascribe to, it must flow through the brand values of the Heavenly Kingdom—peace, love, joy, purity, truth, self-control, generosity, and so forth. We may not wear a physical brand's garment, but our actions are the garb that shows others *who* we serve.

What happens when employees and brand ambassadors don't live out the brand's values? They either get more extensive training or face other consequences, because to a company, the brand, culture, and reputation is everything. The brand is what we immediately see, believe, or feel about a person, product or business.

So, what is the brand resonance that non-believers have of us? Instead of the world thinking that we are hateful, spiteful, judgmental, stingy, closed-off, and crass, they should say of us: "Look how they love one another." "Look how they carry themselves with such joy and peace." "Look how they prioritize their relationships over success." "Look how they give generously without reservation." We get to carry the reputation of all the sacrifices Jesus made on our behalf. He chose us before we could ever choose Him (Ephesians 1:4). He sends us into the world to be His appointed brand ambassadors in a world that doesn't know His name. Are we carrying His Heavenly brand well in our workplace, business, home life, and community?

Pause & Reflect:

Reflect on the concept of being a brand ambassador for Jesus. In the business world, brand ambassadors who don't align with the brand's values may undergo training or face consequences. How can you engage in ongoing spiritual "training" to better represent Jesus in your daily life?

Consider ways to enhance their perception by showcasing the love, joy, and generosity that characterize the brand of Jesus. How can you intentionally build positive brand resonance in your workplace, relationships, and community?

Pattern of Good Works

*In all things showing yourself to be a **pattern** of good works; in doctrine showing integrity, reverence, incorruptibility, sound speech that cannot be condemned, that one who is an opponent may be ashamed, having nothing evil to say of you.*

– Titus 2:7-8 NKJV

Typos

Pattern, model, example, type, a visual form to be copied, such as in crafting an idol; by extension: a pattern of behavior to be emulated

Brene Brown (2018), in her book *Dare to Lead*, shares insight into living out your values in leadership, work, and life: "Living into our values means that we do more than profess our values, we *practice* them. We walk our talk—we are clear about what we believe and hold important, and we take care that our intentions, words, thoughts, and behaviors align with those beliefs."

Titus 2:7-8 calls us to be intentional about the pattern we display, emphasizing the significance of our character, integrity, speech, and conduct. Consider the pattern you show in your personal and professional life that showcase your values.

Are you diligent, honest, and committed? Or are you inconsistent, unreliable, and dishonest? How we handle responsibilities, tasks, and challenges is a testament to our character and values. God sees what others don't. Let your actions speak of your dedication to excellence, reflecting the goodness of the One you serve.

The Greek/Hebrew word *typos* reminds us that we can become a model or example to others as well, that they can start to emulate and take after our patterns and values, whether good or bad. We can choose to be a model that inspires and mirrors the love, creativity, integrity, and grace found in Jesus, or quite the opposite.

As you go about your day or week, ponder your patterns of character, integrity, speech, and conduct. Make a list of areas you would like to improve upon, or habits you would like God to help you break or implement.

Let your life be a visual representation of the truths and values you hold dear. Through practice, consistency, and the help of the Holy Spirit you can become a model for others that is so compelling that even those who oppose you find themselves silenced, unable to speak ill of your character.

Pause & Reflect:

What positive or negative patterns do you currently display in your personal and professional life? Are these patterns aligning with the values you hold dear?

How can you become a positive model or example to others in your sphere of influence? Reflect on the impact your patterns may have on those around you?

Basketfuls of Good

*In Joppa there was a disciple named Tabitha (in Greek her name is Dorcas); she was **always** doing good and helping the poor.*

– Acts 9:36 NIV

Pleres

full, basketfuls, full of, always, basketfuls, covered with

Everyone wants to be known for something. What do you want to be known for? In our current day and age there are countless blogs and tips on developing a personal brand that is unique and memorable. A personal brand is all about your reputation. It's a combination of your skills, values, accomplishments and personal mission that makes you stand out. Personal branding reminds us that everything we do, whether good or bad, is stored up over the course of our lives.

In Acts 9, we learn about Tabitha, who had a strong "personal brand" in her community. She is described as being known for her "good works and acts of charity" (ESV), always doing good. She was also a disciple of Jesus. And when she died, the widows of her community mourned her and sent urgently for Peter (Acts 9:38 NIV). She left a big gap in her community and left many good works behind.

In fact, the Greek/Hebrew word used in this context, *pleres*, translates to basketfuls of good! She had stored up so many good works that the widows of the community who were grieving over her death brought all the robes and fine clothes she had made to show Paul. However, within minutes of prayer God brought Tabitha back to life (Acts 9:40-43). The news spread, and many people came to believe in the Lord as a result.

What can we learn from this? Well, in just a few verses about Tabitha we can glean that she was influential, generous, kind, and used her creativity and skills to help the poor as an outpouring of God's love in her. She was always doing good works - she was a basketful of good works. This shows us what and who she valued.

Could someone get a snapshot of your values, mission and what's in your good works "basket"? Could someone gather a collection of all your good works and bring them to your funeral to show others? Let us take inspiration from Tabitha, and countless other disciples in Scripture, who gave their life to helping others.

Pause and reflect:

Reflect on the qualities mentioned about Tabitha—being influential, generous, kind, and using her skills to help the poor. How can you incorporate these qualities into your own life and interactions? What steps can you take to store up basketfuls of good works and acts of charity in your community?

Consider the concept of a personal brand and how it relates to your reputation, skills, values, and personal mission. Reflect on your interactions in various aspects of life—work, community, and daily commitments. What snapshot of your values and mission could someone gather from those interactions?

Spur One Another

Spur one another on to good works.

– Hebrews 10:24

Paroxysmon
Stimulation, provocation, irritation

Spurs arc mctal riding aids designed for directing the movement of an animal (mainly horses), that you are riding. Cowboys often wear them on their riding boots to gently urge the horse forward and even guide their direction or movement. A good rider knows not to use these for punishment, but more so as an aid of communication.

I find it quite interesting that spur is the word used in Hebrews 10:24, which translates to *paroxysmon* in Greek/Hebrew, meaning to stimulate, provoke or even irritate someone to take action or move forward. So quite literally, in our relationships with one another, we should encourage others to do the good works God is calling them to, to stay on path their purpose, and to pursue righteousness in all things - almost to the point of irritation! Reminding each other daily, "Do your good work! Finish that project! Don't quit! Keep going! If God called you He'll get you through it". And if we hear enough of this day in and day out, it will stimulate us to take action!

We are all prone to wandering, getting distracted, getting frustrated when we encounter obstacles, or forgetting

God's truths and commands to do what He called us to do. We are all tempted to let excuses pile up and be passive bystanders. But we each have the responsibility of provoking one another to stay on track with whatever is in our hands to do and take action. We need people who will be gentle but honest and persistent in reminding us to do our good work and continue on our God-given path.

Accountability and encouragement are key to fulfilling the assignments and purposes God has given us to do! We need each other to stay on track and take action when God calls us to do something. We can't do it alone. So, do you have the right people beside you, spurring you on?

Pause & Reflect:

Are you effectively encouraging and spurring others to take action and fulfill their calling or good works?

Who can you reach out to this week to hold you accountable to stay on track with something God is calling you to do - even when things get tough or you face obstacles?

Use your Gifts

For as in one body we have many members, and the members do not all have the same function, so we, though many, are one body in Christ, and individually members one of another. Having gifts that differ according to the grace given to us, let us use them.

– Romans 12:4-6 ESV

Charisma

Gracious gift:– gifts, gracious favor, spiritual gift

God brought it to my attention one day that a good portion of the letters Paul wrote were written to encourage, uplift, teach, and minister to *other* believers. That means our gifts and good works aren't just for non-believers but also for those within the Church.

Romans 12:4-6 says that we are all a part of the same body but have different functions. God has given each one of us differing *charisma*, which translates to favor and spiritual gifts. That means the gifts, passions, and vocational callings God has given me by His Grace are different than yours! Yet, we co-exist as one, attached to the same Source of grace and power.

Consequently, we need each other. We need other believers to see the gifts in us, to help us refine them, and then use them! No matter what gifts we have, we have a unique part and function in God's greater purpose and plan. So don't compare, or resent, or dismiss your part—or anyone else's—in the Body of Christ. You matter and have God's favor. The point is not what body part or how many gifts we have, but that we discover and *use* them, as verse 6 says. Not sure what your gifts and interests are? I didn't either for a long time! The best advice I would give someone is to start serving somewhere, *anywhere.*

Start by getting involved in a community project, a church ministry that pulls at your heart strings, a project that inspires you, start a new hobby that interests you with other friends or believers. I assure you, once you start God will put you exactly where you're supposed to be to be a blessing to others. He can do a lot more with your messy action than you think, and how will you know what's for you unless you give it a shot?

Pause & Reflect:

Reflect on the benefits of doing life with other Christians. How has your faith and personal growth been impacted by the presence of other believers in your life? Are there specific instances where someone's encouragement or recognition of your gifts has inspired you to grow and serve better?

Explore the idea that each believer has a unique part and function in God's greater purpose. How can you embrace and celebrate the diversity of gifts within the body of Christ, both in yourself and in others? In what ways can you foster an environment that encourages everyone to use their gifts to serve, glorify God, and love one another?

Thoroughly Equipped

All Scripture is God-breathed and is useful for teaching, rebuking, correcting and training in righteousness, so that the servant of God may be ***thoroughly equipped*** *for every good work.*

– 2 Timothy 3:16-18 NIV

Exartizo/artios
Fully equipped; to complete, finish; to furnish perfectly; to finish, accomplish/ capable, proficient, able to meet all demands

When God called me out of running my own business and eventually into nursing, the transition into school felt surprisingly easy. Having no prior experience in the medical field compared to my classmates, I could have let that discourage me, but instead I let it fuel me to be the best. I knew God wanted me there, and He would help me every step of the way. He reminded me that for years I had been in training, and He had equipped me for this new assignment. All those years of instability, the difficult clients, juggling multiple projects and jobs, and investing in my growth led to fruitfulness and an increased ability to meet various demands.

You see, God's intention for us is to be *exartizo artios*, which in Greek/Hebrew translates to fully or *perfectly* furnished, prepared, capable, and equipped for *every* good work. That means any kind of work He calls you to, He is equipping you for it. In my experience the only way to become fully equipped and furnished is for God to first clean out and strip away what is not useful, to make room for what is.

Will we sometimes be unprepared, unequipped, or fearful? Of course! But this is what training is all about and God's grace never runs out. We aren't just training for jobs, we are training for righteousness. We are training to bear much fruit and be useful in God's Kingdom. So today, let God's Word and Spirit furnish your heart, mind, and soul, and let Him prepare you for your next assignment.

Pause & Reflect:

Consider a recent situation where you felt unprepared or caught off guard. How might relying on the wisdom and guidance from the Word of God have influenced your response or perspective in that moment?

Reflect on the concept of being fully equipped for every good work in your life. What practical steps can you take to allow the Word of God to continually furnish and prepare you for the challenges and opportunities ahead?

Overflowing

And God is able to make all grace abound to you, so that in every way, always, having all sufficiency, you may ***abound*** *in every good work.*

– 2 Corinthians 9:8 NIV

Perisseuo

to have abundance, more than enough, overflow, to have an excessive amount of something, ranging from moderate excess to a very great degree of excess

Do you notice the extremes in this verse? *All, every way, always, every*. When we are lacking, God is overflowing and making His grace abound in us and through us to be sufficient, get the job done *and* be generous in our pursuits. We will basically be overflowing.

You see, sometimes we may feel unequipped, lacking in confidence, resources, faith, or knowledge. And how often do we go to the other extreme, using words like; *nothing, never, not enough*. Maybe you have a goal you're working toward, or a new position that is stretching you. Are you questioning yourself, your ability, or if you're in the right place? What if God is saying, "Don't quit doing good, just ask me for more grace!" He is able to give you all you need in *all* scenarios so you can abound in *every* good work and *every* season! We just have to ask!

The Greek/Hebrew word for "abound" here is *perisseuo* which depicts the image of having so much overflow and abundance that there are even leftovers. Superflous! So, if God blesses us with more than enough to do the work we are called to, let us keep on working, giving, serving, praying, and not hoard or keep it all to ourselves, because He promises to keep on giving and giving so that there's plenty to go around.

Continually, the word "sufficiency" shows up, and translates to *autarkeia*, which gives us the picture of a man with perfect independence, able to stand alone. Another way to put it is, contentment, which arises from the full supply of all our needs by God. It's a reminder that if we place all our trust upon God for everything we need, we will be "perfect and lacking nothing" (Philippians 4:11). So today, instead of being focused on where you're lacking, turn your eyes to Jesus who lacks nothing, and loves us enough to help us so we can abound and give all the glory to Him alone.

Pause & Reflect:

Consider a recent challenge or endeavor where you felt lacking or uncertain. How could the concept of God making His grace abound in you bring assurance and confidence in those moments?

Reflect on the idea of sufficiency and contentment. How can you cultivate a mindset of trusting in God's abundance and sufficiency, even when you might feel insufficient or lacking in certain areas?

The Great Finisher

The LORD will perfect that which concerns me; Your mercy, O LORD, endures forever; Do not forsake the works of Your hands.

– Psalm 138:8 AMPC

Gamar

to bring to an end; fulfill; vindicate

God cares about what we care about, even more so! He knows the longing of our souls, the unfinished business, the dreams that keep us up at night, the things we have yet to do, the people we have yet to become. And He promises that He will not forsake us or the *good* work He has begun in our lives. God is the Great Finisher – He finishes what He starts and won't stop until it's perfect.

Other translations of the verse above say, "The LORD will fulfill his purpose for me;" ESV or "The LORD will work out his plans for my life" NLT. The word *perfect* translates to *gamar* meaning "to bring to an end, to fulfill." I may not be the best finisher of projects, in fact, I am way better at starting things then completing them, but thank God He is!

So, if you're worried that you'll miss the boat of opportunities or not fulfill the purposes He has for you, I hope this is an encouragement to you that He will not forsake or abandon you in the process. He is faithful to carry out the work He has started in you, and the plans he has for you. He is the perfector of our faith (Hebrews 12:2).

You won't miss what He has for you! Nor will He call you to something and abandon you halfway or begin a process in you that He won't complete. We can echo what Paul says, "I am confident of this, that the one who began a good work among you will bring it to completion by the day of Jesus Christ" (Philippians:16 NIV).

If this is the case, how can we be active in the work and process God is doing in us? How can we be open minded, open handed, and willing to say yes? We don't want to take a lax approach, believing God will do it all for us while we sit back and relax, because it still takes two to tango, after all. God invites us to be a part of this good work; we are co-working with Him. So, let us carry on!

Pause & Reflect:

Reflect on the reassurance that God cares deeply about the longing of your soul, your dreams, and the unfinished business in your life. How does the promise that God will not forsake the work He has begun in your life bring comfort and encouragement to you? In what specific areas of your life do you need to trust the Great Finisher?

Consider the emphasis on God fulfilling His purpose and working out His plans for your life. How does this perspective shift your approach to opportunities given to you and the fear of missing out on God's purpose for you? How can you actively align yourself with God's purposes and participate in the work He invites you into?

Be Strong

Yet now **be strong**, *Zerubbabel,' says the LORD; 'and* **be strong**, *Joshua, son of Jehozadak, the high priest; and* **be strong**, *all you people of the land,' says the LORD, 'and work; for I am with you,' says the LORD of hosts.*

– Haggai 2:4 ESV

Chazaq

to give strength, repair, encourage; to grasp, seize, hold; to make repairs; to establish oneself firmly; to encourage, to rally strength

Is there a specific thing that God has pressed into your heart to do that you're resisting? One that seems to whisper, "Let's get to work"? Maybe this project, idea or opportunity has not left you since it's conception, and it seems to boomerang back into your mind even after trying to push it away. If so, what's holding you back? Is it fear? Comparison? Uncertainty? Lack of time, resources, or experience? The list could go on of reasons not to begin.

But notice this verse says to be strong three times! The word strong here gives the depiction of rallying up and grasping for strength while standing firm in the face of obstacles or challenges. For a bit of context, the Prophet Haggai sought to challenge and encourage the Jews after their many years of exile because they were experiencing both internal and external opposition and resistance to the project of rebuilding God's temple.

The people of Judah had misplaced their priorities, being more concerned with their own interests than what God was calling them to. They were also discouraged because they knew how beautiful and richly decorated the former temple that Solomon had built was and that their temple would not even compare.

With Haggai's exhortation, the Jews turned from their ways and committed to rebuilding God's temple anew. God told them, "The latter glory of this house will be greater than...And in this place I will provide peace..." (Haggai 2:9 ESV).

You see, when God calls you to an idea, a project, a job, or a place, He will not leave you or forsake you. We can expect that there will be internal or even external resistance and obstacles but that does not mean we shouldn't begin the work, because God gives us the strength.

The lesson also stands that we should not compare ourselves to those who have come before us and the work they have done as an excuse to not even try! There is room for you at the table, and your obedience to God will bring peace, provision, and blessing. With that being said, it's time to rally up the strength you need to stand firm, and get to work! "The LORD your God is in your midst—a warrior bringing victory" (Zephaniah 3:17 CEB).

Pause & Reflect:

Reflect on the idea of a pressing call from God that you might be resisting. What is holding you back from engaging in the work that seems to persistently return to your thoughts? Identify and explore any fears, comparisons, uncertainties, or perceived limitations that may be hindering your obedience and surrender them to the Lord.

How can you rally up the strength and motivation to begin the work you feel called to start? Are there friends, family members, or people who walked before you that you can consult or even borrow confidence from? Let God lead you and give you strength to the necessary take action.

The Quiet Life

Make it your ambition to lead a quiet life: you should mind your own business and work with your hands, just as we told you, so that your daily life may win the respect of outsiders…

– 1 Thessalonians 4:11,12 NIV

Philotimeomai
To have an ambition, aspire to a goal, eager to do something, strive to bring something to pass

I'm known to be a very ambitious person, often working on five or more projects, aiming for big goals, looking at different ways to add to my bag of skills. Though this ambition is a gift, it often needs to be checked by the Holy Spirit to make sure I'm in alignment with His will and His desires for me and my schedule. If I'm not careful I'll overload my calendar in the name of ambition and goal achievement and forget my *why* and what I'm meant to be doing.

The Greek/Hebrew definition for ambition from the verse above is *philotimeomai* which gives us the picture of someone restlessly eager to bring something to pass, who won't stop until their goal is achieved. And what does Paul tell the Thessalonians to restlessly be on pursuit for? A quiet life.

When I read this, I nearly fell off my chair, because my life looked nowhere near quiet, but often way too full and frantic. I was expecting Paul to say, "Strive to do great things for the Kingdom of God" or, "Strive to accomplish as much as you can before your time is up". But strive for a quiet life? Seems difficult. Upon further study I found that the words "quiet life" here entails a person whose life is full of rest, ease and peace. That sounds like a lovely vacation, but how does this look day-to-day when you're being tugged every which way?

John Calvin puts it this way:

"This, therefore, is the best means of a tranquil life, when everyone, intent upon the duties of his own calling, discharges those duties which are enjoined upon him by the Lord, and devotes himself to these things: while the husbandman employs himself in rural labors, the workman carries on his occupation, and in this way everyone keeps within his own limits."

In other words, let us only do the things God has called us to do - nothing less and nothing more. The best way to live a peaceful life is for everyone to focus on and do their own job or responsibilities and stay in their God-given lanes. If everyone did this, my, what the world could look like!

Instead of trying to accomplish everything for everyone, we must instead be so eager and ambitious to protect our schedules, our time, and our energy for only the things God has allowed. Otherwise, we run the risk of burnout and lack of peace, and that is now how God wants us to live.

Whatever God is calling you to say yes to, do it with all of your heart because you are still called to work hard. But don't let unchecked ambition wreak havoc on your basic callings and priorities like faith, family, friends, or fitness.

Whether your goals for life are big and lofty or small and modest, there is something sacred to leading a quiet life, minding your own business, focused solely on the path the

Lord has you on. And just remember, there is nothing wrong with ambition, but a quiet and respectable life can also be a great witness to others.

As J. Aaron Gruben (January, 2018) wrote, "The quiet life can also raise society, adorn the gospel, and change the world. I would, in fact, venture to say the quiet life is the most common way God ordained for His people to adorn his gospel."

Pause & Reflect:

Take a moment to examine your current schedule and list your commitments. Are there activities or responsibilities that seem to overextend you or detract from your faith, family, friends or fitness?

How can you realign your ambitions to fit within what God is calling you to do in this season, ensuring that your time and energy are spent on what truly matters to you and Him and discard the rest?

Many Works

Honor her for all that her hands have done, and let her ***works*** *bring her praise at the city gate.*

– Proverbs 31:31 NIV

Maaseh

work, labor, deed, product; something made, something done

The Proverbs 31 Woman is often lifted up as the epitome of Biblical womanhood and I'd like to show you the good works she did, which were her worship and ministry to the Lord and others!

In the bustling marketplace of her time, she was not merely praised for her domestic skills or business knowledge but for the depth of her character and the impact of her actions. As we explore the Greek/Hebrew word *maaseh*, which encompasses a wide array of activities and endeavors, we see that her life was a tapestry woven with acts of love, hospitality, business, and creativity.

Now the word work here translates to a whole host of things that you and I can feel confident in doing. Here's where *maaseh* shows up throughout Scripture and what it translates to in other passages:

Woven
Occupation
Baking
Design

Handiwork
Construction
Fruit/Crops
Perfumes
Projects

For the Proverbs 31 Woman, whether it was managing her household or engaging in commerce, she approached her work with diligence and integrity. She didn't merely go through the motions; she invested herself fully, recognizing that her work was not just a means of provision but an opportunity to glorify God.

Her baking wasn't just about sustenance; it was a labor of love, nourishing her family and guests with warmth and hospitality. Her designs weren't simply aesthetic; they reflected her creativity and attention to detail, whether in clothing her family or beautifying her surroundings. Her handiwork extended beyond the confines of her home, reaching out to those in need and making a difference in the lives of others. Whether it was constructing shelters, tending to crops, or creating works of art, she used her skills and resources to bless those around her.

Even in the seemingly mundane tasks of life, she found purpose and significance. Every endeavor was infused with meaning, rooted in her devotion to God and her commitment to serving others.

So be encouraged! Whatever occupation or work you find yourself doing can bring glory to God! As we reflect on the example of the Proverbs 31 woman, let's not be overwhelmed by unattainable standards or discouraged by comparison. Instead, let's draw inspiration from her character and the tangible expressions of her faith through work. Let's embrace the diverse talents and passions that God has entrusted to us, knowing that our work, whatever form it may take, can be a beautiful offering of worship and ministry to the Lord and others.

Pause and Reflect:

As you consider the diverse talents and passions described in the Proverbs 31 woman's life, which aspects resonate most deeply with you? How might you leverage your unique gifts and abilities to serve others and glorify God in your daily life?

Reflect on a recent task or project you've undertaken, no matter how small or seemingly insignificant. How can you infuse it with greater purpose and intentionality, viewing it as an opportunity for worship and ministry, just as the Proverbs 31 woman did with her work?

Prosperous Work

Let the favor of the Lord our God be upon us, and ***prosper*** *for us the work of our hands—O prosper the work of our hands!*

– **Psalm 90:17 NRS**

Kuwn

to be established, be steadfast, be firm, be prepared; to set in place, make secure, to be ready

In a world that often celebrates self-reliance, hustle, and determination as the sole determinants of success, the wisdom in Scripture offers a refreshing reassurance. Psalm 90:17 directs our gaze to God, acknowledging that He is the ultimate source of prosperity and stability in our work endeavors.

Though the world may want you to believe that success is all up to you, your effort, your resources, and your talent, the Word of God reminds us that God is the one who confirms, prepares, and establishes us for the work of our hands. The Greek/Hebrew word *kuwn* emphasizes the act of making ready, of setting in place—a reminder that the outcomes of our labor ultimately rest in God's hands.

As 1 Corinthians 3:6-11 reminds us, our role is similar to planting and watering seeds, while God alone brings about the growth. This recognition humbles us, shifting our focus from self-dependence to God-dependence. It calls us to prayerful surrender, trusting in God's timing and sovereignty over the fruit of our efforts.

As St. Ignatius (1968) wisely said, "Pray as though everything depends on God. Work as though everything depends on you". This paradox sums up the essence of faith-filled labor—where we diligently pursue our work while acknowledging God's providential care and guidance.

Our earnest prayer, then, should not solely be for success or prosperity in our work, but for God to be central in all that we do. When we keep God at the forefront, we find ourselves firmly established and secured, regardless of the outcomes of our work.

So, as we embark on each day's work, let us trust, hope, work, and wait with expectant hearts. Let us cultivate a posture of reliance on God's providence, knowing that He alone can establish and prosper the work of our hands. May our labor be an offering of faith and obedience, yielding to God's perfect plan and purposes.

Pause & Reflect:

In what areas of your life are you relying solely on your efforts, resources, or talents for success? How can you shift your perspective to trust in God's role as the one who establishes and prospers your endeavors?

In what ways can you bring your work before God, seeking His guidance and favor? How can you cultivate a right relationship with God as the necessary ingredient for a worthwhile and purposeful life?

Meaningless

*So what do people get in this life for all their hard work and anxiety? Their days of labor are filled with pain and grief; even at night their minds cannot rest. It is all **meaningless**.*

– Ecclesiastes 1:3-4 NLT

Hebel

Breath, vapor, something with no substance, meaninglessness, worthlessness, vanity, emptiness, futility.

Sometimes an existential crisis hits you when you least expect it, as you're sipping your coffee on a Friday morning. Like, "What is the point to everything I do and who am I doing it for?" It's completely normal to question the status quo, to question why we strive for more, getting wrapped up in the rat race and overcommitting when we are barely hanging on by a thread. But these questions, I believe are the Holy Spirit's nudges, a reminder to pause, to take inventory, to re-prioritize. Ecclesiastes is riddled with all sorts of questions about life, work, success and what's truly important.

As King Solomon penned, "Everything is meaningless, utterly meaningless!" (Ecclesiastes 1:2 NLT). I like to think that maybe even Solomon had an existential crisis of his own. He was the wisest man that ever lived, and also the richest during his time. As he neared the end of his life, he began to reflect on all that he had learned along the way.

Solomon had it all, yet he discovered that it was hollow and futile: "But as I looked at everything I had worked so hard to accomplish, it was all so meaningless—like chasing the wind. There was nothing really worthwhile anywhere." (Ecclesiastes 2:11 NLT).

I've heard countless stories of people who reached the pinnacle of success, fame, wealth, or power and once they've arrived they simply can't shake the feeling that it was all for nothing - the sleepless nights, the overworking, the sacrifices. Sadly, many people will often experience this feeling of emptiness and confusion when it comes to their hard work.

This, my friends, is what Solomon means when he says, "chasing after the wind" (Ecclesiastes 2:10-11 ESV). It illustrates the emptiness that is felt when humans strive to fulfill themselves apart from God - you can't contain a breeze, and you never will. A life without God will only get us so far and in the end, it gets us to the end of ourselves. This is where we realize no amount of money, material objects, popularity or approval can get us what we so desperately need and crave - Jesus.

The word meaningless shows up 38 times in the book of Ecclesiastes. The word translates to *hebel* in Greek/Hebrew, which means breath, emptiness, futile. What Solomon was trying to tell us is that all the business endeavors, relationships, music, delicious food, and fine clothing were worthless apart from God, who is the Giver of all these good things in the first place. When it comes to all of our hard work, we must remember the bigger picture.

We do not work for work's sake like the rest of the world chasing and striving anxiously after the wind. We work for the Lord and His sake, and everything we have is a gift from Him, to be used for His glory and the betterment of others.

With that being said, it can be tempting to think in black and white terms about work - that because Ecclesiastes says it's all meaningless we should not care to apply ourselves, work hard, or ever try to succeed. There's this belief in some Christian circles that we should not care about the physical or material at all.

But my belief is that, yes; Without God, everything is meaningless, but *with* God, He infuses whatever we do with colors of meaning, because everything we do is now done to the glory of Him, not just for our own selfish gain.

We do not worship the things we have or accomplish; we worship the Giver who gives them. It's both/and. So please don't despise hard work, or pursuing after the things God has placed in your heart for a reason. Instead, fulfill your earthly responsibilities *and* invite God in to show you that you can have meaning in whatever you do.

Pause & Reflect:

How can you embrace the truth that, as a Christian, you no longer work by the world's value system but for the Lord and His sake? In what ways can your work become a form of worship, done with integrity and in alignment with God's priorities?

How can you navigate the both/and approach, recognizing the importance of earthly responsibilities while expressing the priorities and values of God's kingdom in your everyday activities?

Belief First

Then they said to him, "What must we do, to be doing the works of God?" Jesus answered them, "This is the work of God, that you ***believe*** *in him whom he has sent."*

– John 6:28-29 ESV

Pisteuo

to believe, put one's faith in, trust in, surrender, with an implication that actions based on that trust may follow

In John 6, Jesus' disciples and a crowd of people were following him and had seen a variety of miracles done. After all these miracles and good works they saw Jesus do, they may have felt unsure about what exactly *they* were supposed to be doing to please God. They must have wanted some clear-cut plan, or copy-paste template so they could make sure they were doing it right religiously. But what is interesting is that instead of Jesus giving them a bullet point list of good works to adhere to, He instead gives them *one* main work: to believe in Him. He wanted to make sure they truly understood the essence of why they were doing good works and for whom.

The word *believe* may sound like simple work, but this is more than just an intellectual acknowledgement. The word translates to *pisteuo* in Greek/Hebrew which actually means to put one's faith in, to rely on something with your whole being. To surrender completely to someone else's leadership. And when we believe in the One whom God has sent, we will be moved to take some positive action in our work and our lives. But belief must come first, action second.

Otherwise, we get stuck in a cycle of doing and accomplishing to appease a religion and people's expectations, to seek validation, to prove we are worthy, and all along, forgetting that's not God's desire for us.

Jesus doesn't want us to do anything for Him without first having a complete transformation in our belief system. He doesn't want a transactional relationship, nor does He need our good works. No, He wants an all-encompassing belief: mind, body, spirit. That's why He says, "Now go away and learn the meaning of this verse of Scripture, 'It isn't your sacrifices and your gifts I want—I want you to be merciful.'" (Matthew 9:13 TLB). And in the Old Testament, God says, "I don't want your sacrifices—I want your love; I don't want your offerings—I want you to know me" (Hosea 6:6 TLB).

When we believe *who* Jesus says He is, when we believe what He has done for us, When we believe *where* He is taking us when He returns, it transforms us. The good works that follow this transformational belief will be different than what would have resulted without it. This belief will change our work ethic, how we manage and steward our time and our resources, how we treat people, and whether or not we try to cut corners, cheat, steal, or lie to get ahead. It will change our priorities, our motivations, our attitudes. This all-encompassing, transformational belief will change us first and then everything that follows. *This* is the work of God.

Pause & Reflect:

Consider the concept of belief as presented in the passage, moving beyond mere intellectual acknowledgment to a whole-hearted surrender and reliance on Jesus. How might prioritizing belief first, before action, lead to a deeper alignment with God's purposes and priorities in your work and relationships?

Roll your Works

Commit your work to the LORD, and your plans will be established.

– Proverbs 16:3 ESV

Galal
to roll down, roll away; to commit, turn over

Are you someone who likes to control everything? Maybe you're training someone else at work, and you expect them to do it your way, so you watch their every move. Or, maybe you're the person who never asks for help with a project because you don't trust anyone else to do it as well as you. One of the things I love about this Christian walk is that we are works in progress, and God loves to teach us a better approach to what we are used to.

I say, "I love control." God says, "Give me control".

I say, "I don't trust anyone." God says, "Trust me above all others."

I say, "Here's my perfect plan." God says, "Entrust your plans to me, and I will perfect them."

In the verse above, we are invited to commit our work to the Lord. The word commit translates to *galal* in Greek/Hebrew, which means to roll away or turn over. It gives us the image of physically rolling something onto someone else. This powerful visual gives us a sense of relief and ease, knowing that the person we are rolling this burden or work onto is going to take good care of it!

And if something isn't beneficial for us or aligns with His will, we can trust that He will guide us and even shape our thoughts and desires. But we must remain open-handed, open-hearted, and open-minded. Because sometimes, even when we roll our works, burdens, hopes, and dreams onto God, there's no guarantee that our plans will unfold exactly as we envision. But because we serve a good God, we can trust Him to handle our lives and plans better than we ever could. Ultimately, we can have confidence that He will work all things out for our good and His glory (Romans 8:28).

Pause & Reflect:

Are there areas in your life where you find it challenging to relinquish control over the outcome, or you're tempted to be a perfectionist? How can you shift to inviting God into whatever you're gripping and start to open your hands with it, instead?

Visualize the act of rolling your works and burdens onto God: what emotions come up? In what specific areas of your life can you actively roll, commit, and entrust your work to God? How might this act of entrusting bring a sense of ease and assurance?

What Sparks Joy?

The LORD directs the steps of the godly. He ***delights*** *in every detail of their lives.*

– Psalm 37:23 NLT

Hapes

to desire, delight in, be pleased with, have pleasure

The Oscar winning movie, *Chariots of Fire* is the story depicting Eric Liddell's life as a Scottish Olympic athlete and person of deep faith. In responding to the dichotomy between choosing the work of an Olympic athlete or serving as a foreign missionary, Liddell (1981) said, "I believe God made me for a purpose, but he also made me fast. And when I run I feel His pleasure."

What a joy that the God of the universe delights in us and every detail of our lives. He has given us the ability to feel joy, excitement, fulfillment, and satisfaction in various types of work, hobbies or passions.

What makes *you* happy? It's a simple question, yet sometimes we fear the answer because it's not practical, or sometimes we feel guilt for feeling joy, so we stuff it down. But within joy and holy delight lies a window into some sort of divine purpose set before us. Just like Liddel, God has given us passions and skills waiting to be unwrapped and shared with others. He loves our joy when we've painted a masterpiece, when we sell our first product, when we lose track of time doing what we love.

He never misses a beat, and He delights in us when we are filled with holy delight for the things He's given us to steward. To love what we do, and do it will all our might, is to honor Him. He isn't just delighted in us when we serve in church, donate money, or sit in church pews - He delights in *all* the details of our lives when we live for Him.

Reading our Bibles, attending church, and serving are only 10-20% of our lives, but what about the rest? Guess what! God cares about the other 80% as well. Don't let anyone discredit your faith or joy because of the work you love to do, or the things you're passionate about, as some did to Liddel, accusing him of no longer caring for God. His beautiful response was that to *not* run would dishonor God. Let that settle in!

We need more Christians who are lit up with excitement and delight when they do the things they love. Isn't it ironic, the Greek/Hebrew word *hapes* sounds and looks like happy! We get to make God happy, while we are happily doing the projects, hobbies, and jobs that fill our days. That honors Him!

Pause & Reflect:

Are there specific moments or accomplishments in your life that have brought you great joy and fulfillment? How can you recognize and celebrate these moments as God's good gifts to you?

How can you invite God into the daily routines, work, and leisure activities? In what ways can you cultivate joy and delight in various aspects of your life, recognizing them as opportunities to experience and share God's goodness?

Satisfaction

I know that there is nothing better for people than to be happy and to do good while they live. That each of them may eat and drink, and find satisfaction in all their toil—this is the gift of God.

– Ecclesiastes 3:12-13 NIV

Tob

good, pleasing, desirable; goodness; this can refer to quality as well as to moral goodness:– good, better, best, well, fine, prosperity

The words of Ecclesiastes remind us of a profound truth: true satisfaction in our work is not found in the fleeting pleasures of worldly success but in recognizing that our work is a gift from God. The Greek/Hebrew word *tob* encapsulates this idea beautifully, describing not only the quality of our work but also the moral goodness inherent in fulfilling our God-given purpose and assignments.

When we approach our work with a mindset focused on its goodness, purpose, and potential for impact, we begin to experience a shift in perspective. Each task, no matter how mundane or challenging, becomes an opportunity to glorify God and serve others. Whether we're flipping burgers, crunching numbers, teaching children, or caring for the sick, our work takes on new meaning when we view it as sacred.

Finding satisfaction in our work doesn't mean that every moment will be easy or enjoyable. There will be days of exhaustion, frustration, and doubt. Yet, even in the midst of the mundane, we can still find joy. We can access solace in knowing that our efforts aren't in vain if we trust in God to help us day to day. We can make an impact by doing good right where we are, with all that we have.

Moreover, if we do not currently find satisfaction or joy in the work we are doing, let us ask God for wisdom to find the work that truly lights us up. As Dale Carnegie says, "People rarely succeed unless they have fun in what they're doing." It's much harder to seize the day when we dread what we do, but time does pass by more quickly when we are having fun. Sure, there are things we need to do, responsibilities to heed to, but what about making margin for more fun? For joy? For laughter and enjoyment? This is also a gift from God.

In the end, true satisfaction in our work is not found in the praise of men or the size of our paycheck, but in God who gives us the ability to wake up each day and fulfill our assignments joyfully. And if we haven't found the work that lights us up, ask God to show you where you can fit in some good old enjoyment. All of this is indeed a precious gift from God.

Pause & Reflect:

Consider a time when you felt dissatisfied or unfulfilled in your work. How might embracing gratitude and humility have transformed your experience? What steps can you take to cultivate a deeper sense of holy satisfaction in your current work or circumstances?

As you reflect on your own work and daily tasks, how can you make room for more joy and fun? If you're unsure, just ask God to surprise you!

Work with Love

If I have the gift of prophecy and understand all mysteries and all knowledge, and if I have all faith so that I can move mountains but do not have love, I am nothing.

– 1 Corinthians 13:2

Agape

Love, in the NT usually the active love of God for his Son and his people, and the active love his people are to have for God, each other, and even enemies

Love is one of the most powerful good works we are called to. It is the first of the fruits of the Spirit. It is what Christ followers should showcase on an ongoing basis. Receiving the abundant, unconditional, perfect, eternal love of God must come first. And once we experience and internalize this type of love, it will pour out of us like a stream, and be the true mark and flag of our homes, our words, or work, our very lives. 1 John 4:19 NIV says, "We love because He first loved us."

Love is the lifeblood of our walk with Jesus. For some, love comes easier than others, but regardless, we can't always love in our own strength. We need the power of the Holy Spirit to do the miraculous: love or forgive those who are hurting, who are difficult, or even those who are against us. Love comes before status, success, and knowledge. Without love, it says, we are nothing (1 Corinthians 13:2).

If we have all the riches, influence, powers to heal, ability to discern the most complex mysteries, or successfully lead thousands to Christ, without love we are *nothing*. Empty. It does not add to our salvation, or our standing with God. Truly, He doesn't need more of our works, but more of our devotion and our hearts. Humility is what allows love to act. As Jesus says in John 13:34-35 NIV, "A new command I give you: Love one another. As I have loved you, so you must love one another. By this everyone will know that you are my disciples, if you love one another."

If this is the commandment that fulfills the law, let's start there and go back there every time we forget. Our good works must come as an overflow of this perfect love, not precede it. When it doesn't make sense to love, help, serve, give, and commit. That's when Christians should be the first to step up to the plate. As Felix (1989) said, "We do not speak of great things. We do them!"

Love is an action, not just a warm fuzzy feeling. Love is how we treat customers, clients, employees, coworkers, family members, and those who are very different from us. And sometimes, love stretches us and our boundaries, forgetting about our rights, positions, and needs. But that's what Jesus' love did for us. He is the very definition of love. So, let our love be so ripe that anyone who tastes it will see and experience Love Himself.

Pause & Reflect:

How has experiencing and internalizing God's abundant, unconditional love impacted your ability to love others? Consider the impact that working from this love can have on your work and daily life.

What is the implication of love being an action, rather than just words and warm, fuzzy feelings? How can we get back to the true meaning of this type of love and follow in Jesus' footsteps?

A Mind to Work

So we built the wall. And all the wall was joined together to half its height, for the people had a ***mind*** *to work.*

– Nehemiah 4:6 ESV

Leb
heart; by extension: the inner person, self, the seat of thought and emotion: conscience, courage, mind, understanding

Sometimes God calls us to a specific assignment or work that is less than pleasant. I've been called to jobs or assignments where I felt completely unqualified and had to rise to the occasion. I've also been in positions or seasons where I was overqualified, underpaid and often overlooked.

In both of those seasons, I really had to get my mind right with the Lord to show up with excitement and passion for every day, even when it was hard, mundane, or frustrating. I knew if I didn't pay attention to my thoughts and attitudes, they would quickly steer me to comparison, disappointment, and envy of others. Ultimately how we choose to show up and do our work, and whether we have a "mind to work", is a matter of the heart and the thoughts we allow.

The word “mind” in Nehemiah 4:6 translates to the Greek/Hebrew word *leb* which means the inner person, the heart, or the seat of thought and emotion. Other verse translations say that the people were excited, determined, or eager to work. In other words, Nehemiah and the people were filled with such deep seated excitement, passion and determination to fulfill their assignment for God, they weren’t going to let anything internally or externally get in their way.

Nehemiah was a Jewish leader who played a crucial role in the rebuilding of Jerusalem after the Babylonian exile. Nehemiah was a high-ranking leader who had it all and was most likely comfortable in his position. Until he hears about the destruction of Jerusalem's walls.
That’s when he felt God calling him to return to Jerusalem and rebuild its walls. This assignment was not an easy one - many people mocked him for having such an absurd goal, and others tried to stop him with threats and attacks, but Nehemiah persisted to the end. He prayed, planned, prepared and delegated to other workers to help in the rebuilding, and within 54 days it was complete, which was an astounding accomplishment done in a short amount of time. Many people were in awe.

What can we learn from Nehemiah and those who rebuilt the walls of Jerusalem? They were stirred in their hearts for a cause they deeply cared about. They were willing to sacrifice comfort, disregard others' opinions, and work consistently despite challenges, relying on the Lord's strength, provision and protection. They remained present in their assignment and were determined to finish. They had a heart and mind to work until it was complete. Maybe for you, it's time to get your heart and emotions aligned, then focus your mind to do the work in front of you with joy, passion and determination for the Lord. Then watch how God shows up to get the glory, and what you'll learn in the midst!

Pause and Reflect:

Consider the obstacles and challenges Nehemiah faced while rebuilding Jerusalem's walls. How do you typically respond to external obstacles or internal doubts when pursuing a God-given task? What can you learn from Nehemiah's determination and reliance on God to help you persevere in your own assignments?

Ministry

*And He Himself gave some to be apostles, some prophets, some evangelists, and some pastors and teachers, for the equipping of the saints for the work of the **ministry**...*

- Ephesians 4:11-12 NKJV

Diakonia

Ministry, service, this can refer to helps and service of various kinds which can range in meaning from "spiritual" biblical teaching (AC 6:4) to the "practical" giving of provisions, supplies, support and finances to those in need (2 Co 9:12)

Often the word *ministry* is a source of confusion for many Christians. Rev. Tim McConnell, the pastor of Peachtree United Methodist Church wrote, "If you have a job in the church, give it up and find a ministry! God doesn't want us feeling stuck with a job, but excited, fulfilled and faithful in a specific ministry" (Mckinney, 2022).

Think about what would happen if all of us quit our current jobs and became Christian missionaries or signed up to work within a church instead. What would happen to a large majority of workplaces without Jesus followers there using their gifts, talents, skills, and experiences? While it is true that some are called, appointed, and commissioned for "spiritual" ministry, like leading a church or teaching the Word, it is also true that many are called, appointed, and commissioned to "practical" ministry like healthcare, education, business, creativity, motherhood, etc.

Pastors and preachers do what *they* are best at so that *we* can do what we're best at: being equipped to do our ministry elsewhere in the world. Most of us are called to an industry or job where pastors, preachers or ministry workers will never be found, and may not even be welcomed, that others of us would have immediate access to because of our our status, resources, reputation, or skill.

During World War II, the Protestant theologian Dietrich Bonhoefer issued a famous statement from his prison cell about ministry (Greek word diakonia) in the Church: "The Church is only the Church when it is there for others. We must, therefore, not forget that we are the capital C Church, and it's not just a physical building. Continually, the image of the *diakonia* is to try to end the hell on earth for many people." (Buttigieg, 2009).

Ephesians 4:11-12 reminds us that the *saints* are being equipped. That's you and me! The term "saint" comes from the word "sanctified," which means "to be set apart for God's service." How powerful is that? We each have a unique ministry and assignment where we get to end "hell" for others and usher in heaven instead! "Every manner of good work has the capacity—by the power of the Spirit—to be a means of participation in God's renewal of the world" (*Theology of Work*).

So, do you have a job or a ministry? It is simple to determine:

> *"If you are doing it just well enough to get by, it's a job.*
> *If you are doing it to the best of your ability, it's a ministry.*
> *If you'll do it as long as it doesn't interfere with other activities, it's a job.*

If you're committed to staying with it, even if it means letting go of other things, it's a ministry.
If you quit because no one praised you or thanked you, it's a job.
If you do it because you know it needs to be done, it's a ministry.
It's hard to get excited about a job. It is almost impossible not to get excited about a ministry.
People may say "well done" when you do your job. The Lord will say "well done" when you complete your ministry.
The average church is filled with people doing jobs. A great church is filled with people involved in ministry."
- Unknown (Mckinney, 2022)

Pause and Reflect:

How do you perceive the role that God has assigned to you in your daily life? Whether it is within your workplace, community, or family, do you see it as a form of ministry where you are serving others and glorifying God?

Take a moment to evaluate if you are merely fulfilling a job or truly engaging in a ministry that brings you excitement, fulfillment, and a sense of purpose. If you're not sure, ask God to lead you to your ministry.

Equal Service

*It would not be right for us to neglect the ministry of the word of God in order to **wait on tables**.*

– Acts 6:2 NIV

Diakoneo

to serve, wait on, help, attend to; this often refers to spiritual and practical ministry in the Church. "To wait upon tables" (Ac 6:2) may mean to literally help in serving food, though some believe it refers (also) to the handling of finances

Let's look at this excerpt written by Dorothy Sayer's "Why Work" essay from Letters to the Diminished Church (1942):

> *Let the Church remember this: that every maker and worker is called to serve God in his profession or trade – not outside it. The Apostles complained rightly when they said it was not meet they should leave the word of God and serve tables; their vocation was to preach the word. But the person whose vocation it is to prepare the meals beautifully might with equal justice protest: It is not meet for us to leave the service of our tables to preach the word. The official Church wastes time and energy, and moreover, commits sacrilege, in demanding that secular*

> *workers should neglect their proper vocation in order to do Christian work – by which She means ecclesiastical work. The only Christian work is good work well done. Let the Church see to it that the workers are Christian people and do their work well, as to God: then all the work will be Christian work, whether it is church embroidery, or sewage farming.*

The Church is called to recognize the value and equality of diverse callings, refraining from viewing some as higher or more spiritual than others. Acts 6:1-7 is often taken out of context, leading to a poor view of other types of work compared to spiritual ministry. The apostles' call to "serve tables" is not a condescending remark but a recognition of the importance of everyone doing the work they are specifically called to, administering to the needs of others. There is a profound lesson here: In God's eyes, no job is trivial or demeaning, and all forms of service can contribute to His purposes when done with excellence.

The original Greek/Hebrew term, *diakaneo*, similar to the previous chapter, translates to "serve," emphasizing the equality of both forms of service. If you continue to read Acts 6:3-5, the apostles called everyone together to delegate the responsibility of resource distribution and assign 7 deacons, "full of faith and the Holy Spirit," illustrating that other types of ministry and work are just as important and impactful when we invite God into our service.

Both are essential in God's mission. "This passage helps us to see that all work that builds the community or, more broadly, that promotes justice, goodness, and beauty, is—

in a deep sense—service (or ministry) to the world" (*Theology of Work*).

So, whether you're a pastor of a church, an English teacher, or a janitor, when you commit to doing your service and ministry with the power of the Holy Spirit, with joy, excellence, and faithfulness, you are doing God's work.

Pause & Reflect:

Reflect on Dorothy Sayers' statement, "The only Christian work is good work well done." How might your approach to your profession change if you view all work as an opportunity to serve God, regardless of its nature or societal status?

Consider the concept of diakoneo, meaning to serve, wait on, and attend to both spiritual and practical needs. How can you integrate this idea into your daily work, recognizing the significance of serving others in your profession and contributing to God's purposes?

God's Will

Pray then like this: "Our Father in heaven, hallowed be your name. Your kingdom come, your will be done, on earth as it is in heaven."

– Matthew 6:9 NIV

Thelema

What one wishes or has determined shall be done; what God wishes to be done by us; will, choice, inclination, desire, pleasure

Often, we know what God's will is, but we have difficulty doing it. We fear discomfort, loss, or suffering when we do the right thing, but God's will is what is ultimately most fulfilling for us, and what also achieves His purposes. His will is to redeem His children and the earth, and for His Kingdom to prevail. The word *will* translates to *thelema* in Greek/Hebrew which has a two-fold meaning: His purposes and wishes that He is determined to do, and what God desires and wishes for us to do.

Thankfully, He has left us a manual - the Bible - which teaches us what his wishes and desires are for our lives. Things like, "Do not lie, do not steal, do not envy, love your neighbor, pray fervently, etc. And also, He has individual "wills" for our lives that we may not find in the Bible but are discovered as we keep in step with the Holy Spirit. As Isaiah 30:21 (ESV) reminds us, "And your ears shall hear a word behind you, saying, 'This is the way, walk in it,' when you turn to the right or when you turn to the left." Examples of this are God calling you to move to a new city, marry a specific person, or pivot careers. Regardless, when we are unsure, we can trust that if we ask for wisdom, He will reveal to us what is good, pleasing, and within His will (James 1:5).

What is most fascinating is that somehow, His ultimate will of what He is determined to do in the world and His individual wills for our lives converge to bring about His perfect, determined plan. It's something we have yet to understand. But even if we do not understand the complexities of all He is doing from beginning to end, we can still participate in doing what is right, good, and honorable. We will be so much better for it, and so will the world.

"When you do anything good and in accordance with God's will, such as acting righteous, noble, or courageous—you feel fulfilled, even when faced with very difficult and painful situations. In short, when we do good (God's will), we are fulfilled; and the more good we do, the more fulfilled we are. When we avoid the good or do things that are not God's will, we feel unfulfilled; and the more we do that, the more empty we feel." (Horse and Chariot, 2023).

So today, how can you be determined to do His will (what pleases Him and what He is calling you to do) and commit to doing just that in your workplace, projects or community?

Pause & Reflect:

What am I absolutely certain is God's will for me to participate in? If I am unsure, how can I approach him to discover what his will might be in a certain situation?

Reflecting on the Lord's Prayer, how can I actively participate in God's ongoing plan to bring His Kingdom to Earth and fulfill His desires?

Greater Works

*Truly, truly, I say to you, whoever believes in me will also do the works that I do, and **greater** works than these will he do, because I am going to the Father.*

– John 14:12 ESV

Meizon
greater, larger, older, louder, more, greatest, all the louder, weightier

Jesus healed the sick, raised the dead, turned water into wine and walked on the surface of water itself. How then, will we do even greater works than these? The Bible says that there are so many good works Jesus did that were not even written, and if they were, "the world itself could not contain the books that would be written" John 21:25 (KJV). The word "greater" translates to the Greek/Hebrew word *meizon* which means "more, bigger, larger, weightier".

While some interpret this as many converts to Christianity, a broader perspective could encompass all forms of meaningful work by all believers everywhere. That means when we work together indwelt by the power of Jesus' Spirit, we accomplish far more in quantity than He did on earth, since His earthly ministry was primarily confined to Galilee and Judea.

As disciples of Jesus we are no longer oblivious to the

divine Masterplan and our purpose on earth, but are now active participants in the world-restoration process, sharing in the intimate relationship and business between the Father and the Son (John 15:14) - what an honor! That means we get to be active contributors by embracing the mission of going into the world, and doing a wide range of good works greater, *or more,* than have been done. But how is this possible?

The answer lies in John 15:5: For apart from Him we can do nothing. The outcome of abiding in God's vine and being powered by His life-giving sap will lend itself to an overflow of productive labor, symbolized by bearing fruit that will last (John 15:16). Does this mean we will all be able to walk on water, raise the dead, and multiply the fish like Jesus did? Not necessarily. No human has surpassed the power or majesty of Jesus' miracles.

However, we do have the same Spirit who raised Jesus from the dead *living* within us, and this same Spirit distributes different gifts to different people (1 Corinthians 12:4) to accomplish greater, weightier and more good works. Jesus also leaves us with a promise of answered prayer. He says, "And I will do whatever you ask in my name, so that the Father may be glorified in the Son. You may ask me for anything in my name, and I will do it" (John 14:13 - 14 NIV).

Therefore, Believers are encouraged to engage in a broad spectrum of good works. This can be anything from teaching kindergartners, to designing homes, to doing surgery, to feeding the poor. The *essence* lies in active service as the embodiment of God's promises and love. Therefore, the work we do is not just as a means of personal fulfillment but an essential aspect of participating in God's ongoing plan for creation and restoration.

Pause & Reflect:

Reflect on the different gifts and talents you have been given. How can you use these unique abilities to contribute to the "greater works" Jesus spoke about, and how can you ensure that these efforts align with the mission of sharing God's love and contributing to His plan for world restoration?

How does this assurance of supernatural support influence your approach to your daily work and the challenges you face? In what ways can you more actively seek and rely on God's guidance to accomplish meaningful and impactful good works in your community?

Work From Rest

Come to me, all who labor and are heavy laden, and I will give you rest. Take my yoke upon you, and learn from me; for I am gentle and lowly in heart, and you will find rest for your souls. For my yoke is easy, and my burden is light.

– Matthew 11:28-30 NIV

Anapauo
to cause or permit one to cease from any movement or labor in order to recover and collect his strength; be refreshed, resting, give rest, take life easy, wait.

One of the good works we are called to as believers is rest. God knew from the beginning of creation that humans would struggle with rest. He gave us an example of taking a break from work on the seventh day (Genesis 2:2-3). In the hustle and bustle of life, Jesus extends a timeless invitation, one that the world cannot give. This is not merely a call for a break from the daily grind, or to have a self-care, Sabbath Sunday, but a profound offer of rest that penetrates the depths of our being - if we let it.

This rest He invites us into is a total mind, body, and soul refreshment without an expensive price-tag. It's an invitation to cease striving in religious labor, or trying to win over His love; it's an invitation to be free from overcommitment and overdoing and to receive His grace.

This is an invitation for refreshment in the very core of our existence.

Imagine a reprieve where, despite the weight of burdens, you can breathe freely, knowing that Jesus is carrying and has carried the load. In the context of Jesus' time and Matthew 11:28-30, a yoke had many uses: a frame placed on animals for pulling various objects; a pair of scales; an oppressed condition, like slavery. Jesus, in offering His yoke, is saying, "I've shouldered the weight for you. The burden of sin, the struggles, the heaviness – I've bore it all, so you never have to." His labor was not in vain; it was the labor of love, setting us free from the enslavement of sin and hell. And He even offers this rest when we are overwhelmed, exhausted and burdened by the demands of life, work and pressures.

What if instead of working *then* resting, we instead work from this place of true rest? What would our work look like then, or our schedules? When we take upon ourselves the yoke that is light and easy, I have a feeling we'll walk around with more freedom and less burnout.

So as you go about your week, remember the unforced rhythms of grace. Don't try to take on more than you can handle, say no if you have to, make time for God's word, for friends and family, exercise and fresh air. The basics. Ask the Holy Spirit what kind of rest you need, be it physical, emotional, spiritual or relational, and then let your work sprout from this place of rest and peace.

And remember friend, don't attempt to reclaim burdens that Christ has already buried. Embrace the freedom He offers, breathe in the rest for your weary soul, mind, or body and find solace in Him. The rest will be taken care of.

Pause & Reflect:

Reflect on the areas of your life where you feel the most burdened or overwhelmed. How can you actively accept Jesus' invitation to rest in these areas? What practical steps can you take to lay down these burdens and embrace the refreshment and ease that Jesus offers?

Consider what the "unforced rhythms of grace" look like in your daily routine or workday. What would it look like to work from a place of rest? How can you ensure you are not overcommitting or striving unnecessarily?

Preach

*And as you go, **preach**, saying, 'The kingdom of heaven has come near.' Heal the sick, raise the dead, cleanse those with leprosy, cast out demons. Freely you received, freely give.*

– Matthew 10:6-8 NIV

Kerysso

to preach, proclaim, tell, often urging acceptance of the message, with warnings of consequences for not doing so

In our attempt to do all the good works God has called us to, with our actions and our hands, let us not forget to share the Good News with our mouths. As 2 Timothy 4:2-5 ESV says, "Preach the word; be prepared in season and out of season; correct, rebuke and encourage—with great patience and careful instruction".

Jesus' instruction is two-fold: go to the lost sheep (unbelievers), and as you go, do good works *and* preach. I love that statement, "as you go", meaning we are all being sent out, wherever we are, whatever we do. If we're believers, we have miracle-working power within us that can flow out of our lives to show that the Kingdom of God is near and *tangible*.

Notice the examples of the good works listed in Matthew 10:8: Heal the sick, raise the dead, cleanse those with leprosy, and cast out demons. In modern times, these good works could look something like this: Serve the poor, treat your patients with the best care, deliver a stellar customer experience, and lead your team with humility. And as you go, preach, saying, "Jesus is alive and near, and He loves you."

There is power in our actions, but there is also power in our words, and so many people around us are desperate for an ounce of truth, to hear words of comfort, and that there is hope, freedom, abundant life, healing on the other side of their darkness. There is power in telling someone that Jesus can meet them where they are, or that you're praying for them, while sending them flowers, or being a shoulder to cry on.

Maybe the preaching you do won't always look the same - in fact, each situation and person may require different words or actions. But when people ask why you are full of peace in your circumstances, or why you're so kind to someone who is rude, or how you handle stress with such peace, you can give them the truth! As 1 Peter 3:15 NIV reminds us, "Always be prepared to give an answer to everyone who asks you to give the reason for the hope that you have. But do this with gentleness and respect".

Preaching doesn't always mean presenting the full gospel in five minutes; it could mean sharing your testimony of what God has done in your situation or sharing scripture that God is using to comfort you. The Holy Spirit will lead you, guide you, and give you the right words at the right time (Luke 12:11,12). Just remember this: the Word of God has the power to transform someone's life. And how will they know of the goodness of God and what Jesus has done for them, if we do not proclaim with our mouths (Romans 10:14)?

Pause & Reflect:

How intentional are you in combining your actions and words to share the message of the Gospel with those around you? Are there areas where you can align your deeds and words more effectively?

Reflect on a time when someone shared the message of the Gospel with you, whether through words, actions, or both. How did it impact your life, and what can you learn from that experience in your own approach to sharing the Good News?

I would love to hear from you!

To write to Lorena Alexandra personally,
or to book her to speak at your church,
conference, or on your podcast, visit her website:

www.lorenaalexandra.com

Bibliography

Alder, Shannon L. *The Narcissistic Abuse Recovery Bible : Spiritual Recovery from Narcissistic and Emotional Abuse*. Springville, Utah, Cfi, An Imprint Of Cedar Fort, Inc, 2018.

"Avodah: A Seamless Life of Work, Worship, and Service." *Institute for Faith, Work & Economics*, 25 Aug. 2015, tifwe.org/avodah-a-life-of-work-worship-and-service/. Accessed 21 Apr. 2024.

Brown, Brené. *Dare to Lead: Brave Work, Tough Conversations, Whole Hearts*. Random House Large Print Publishing, 2018.

Buttigieg, Charles. *"DIAKONIA" in the New Testament Era*. 2009.

Caine, Christine. "Steps of Faith | Small Beginnings." *Www.youtube.com*, 22 Jan. 2024, www.youtube.com/watch?v=3tsSXpRLXMI . Accessed 21 Apr. 2024.

Calvin, John. *Commentaries on the Epistles of Paul the Apostle to The Philippians, Colossians, and Thessalonians*. Baker House Books, Grand Rapids, MI. P 278

Chariots of Fire. Directed by Hugh Hudson, 20th Century Studios, 9 Oct. 1981.

Dillard, Annie. *The Writing Life*. New York, Harper & Row, 1989.

Gruben, J. (2018, January 22). *Aspiring to live the quiet life - J. Aaron Gruben*. J. Aaron Gruben. https://nmgrubens.com/2018/01/quiet-life.html#_edn2

Hinkle, Author Curt. "It's All Greek to Me!" *Practical Theology Today*, 18 June 2019, practicaltheologytoday.com/2019/06/18/its-all-greek-to-me-or-greek-101/. Accessed 10 May 2024.

Horn, Trent. "St. Ignatius Said What?" *Catholic Answers*, 31 July 2019, www.catholic.com/magazine/online-edition/st-ignatius-said-what.

King Jr, Martin Luther. *Loving Your Enemies*. 1957. Sermon.

Lawrence, Brother. *The Practice of the Presence of God : Conversations and Letters of Brother Lawrence*. 1982. Whitaker House, 2009.

Marcus Minucius Felix, et al. *We Don't Speak Great Things-- We Live Them!* Amberson, Pa,

Scroll Pub. Co., 200, 1989.

Mckinney, Russell. "A Job or a Ministry?" *The Disciple's Road*, 14 Oct. 2022, russellmckinney.com/2022/10/14/a-job-or-a-ministry-2/. Accessed 10 May 2024.

"Moral Compass — Teaching of Virtue by Horse & Chariot." *Www.horseandchariot.com*, 24 July 2023, www.horseandchariot.com/moral-compass. Accessed 10 May 2024.

Naber, Andrew. "One Third of Your Life Is Spent at Work." *Gettysburg College*, 2021, www.gettysburg.edu/news/stories?id=79db7b34-630c-4f49-ad32-4ab9ea48e72b. Accessed 21 Apr. 2024.

Pease, Glenn. *Occupations in Heaven*. Sermon, April 9, 2021.

Sayers, Dorothy L. *Letters to a Diminished Church : Passionate Arguments for the Relevance of Christian Doctrine*. 1942. Nashville, Thomas Nelson, 2004.

Smitty. "Word Study: Poieo and Prasso." *Smitty's Thoughts*, 21 Apr. 2010, smittysthoughts.wordpress.com/2010/04/21/word-study-poieo-and-prasso/. Accessed

21 Apr. 2024.

Snodgrass, Ken. "Martin Luther on Vocation (Part I)." *Ken Snodgrass*, 18 Apr. 2022, www.kensnodgrass.com/martin-luther-on-vocation-part-i/. Accessed 21 Apr. 2024.

"Theology of Work Bible Commentary: New Testament." *Theology of Work*, www.theologyofwork.org/new-testament/. Accessed 11 May 2024.

"Titus: Working for Good Deeds." *Theology of Work*, 2015, www.theologyofwork.org/new-testament/pastoral-epistles/titus-working-for-good-deeds/. Accessed 25 Apr. 2024.

Work, Theology of. "Serving the Word and Serving Tables Are Equally Valuable (Acts 6:2-4)." *Theology of Work*, www.theologyofwork.org/new-testament/acts/a-clash-of-kingdoms-community-and-power-acts-5-7/the-spirit-and-the-worker-acts-61-7/serving-the-word-and-serving-tables-are-equally-valuable/. Accessed 10 May 2024.

Made in United States
Troutdale, OR
09/02/2024

22517854R00064